A Year

in the

Life

of a

Poet

2023

Glen Wasson

Introduction

Welcome to my second book of poetry. My first was *New Poetry by an Old Man,* released in July of 2021.That is available from Amazon, Barnes and Noble and other online sellers.

I am a retired mechanical engineer, a one-time linguistic missionary in Sierra Leone West Africa, school bus driver, sawyer of exotic hardwoods, soap salesman, retail salesman and failed business owner. I obtained my BS degree in 1999 and retired at 60. My first wife Sally divorced me after 35 years and I left Wichita, Kansas, for California. On the internet I met my second wife Daisy. We married and moved to Yuma, Arizona. After 20 years Daisy passed away from cancer and I moved into a senior living complex where I met my third wife, Michelle. We have been together for a year and a half and share caring for her dog Bucky.

I was born in Nebraska but have lived at 55 addresses in several states and in Africa. I got my Social Security Card at age 11 and have worked at 35 jobs. All this makes me the man I am and it is through this that I write my poems.

As an engineer I was a "Thing" person, looking down on the liberal arts, but that all changed in 2019 when at the age of 80 I became interested in online classes in literature and philosophy. In 2021 I took a course in poetry and never looked back.

What do you expect in this book of poems? Well you will not find what they taught you in school. This is not contemporary Free Verse, Haiku, or what would be called Modern Poetry. It is not Traditional Poetry with Sonnets, Couplets and Rhymes. The closest you will find is Blank Verse but without the rhymes. There are a few rhymes but are almost by accident.

I have been around music most my life and enjoy the rhythm and meter that you tap your toes to and I carry that into my poetry. English is a Timed-Stressed language in that our words are broken into syllables, some stressed, some unstressed. A stressed syllable will cause your jaw to drop and will be pitched a bit higher and continued a little longer than an unstressed one. A common syllable is called an Iamb (pronounced I am) and consists of an unstressed syllable followed by a stressed syllable to produce a poetic Foot with a beat of "ta Dum". "Today" is an Iambic foot in that it has an unstressed syllable "To" followed by a stressed syllable "day" and is pronounced to-DAY. A poetic line of three Iamb feet in a row would be ta Dum, ta Dum, ta Dum. The stressed syllable is called the Beat and in English we count the stressed beats, not the syllables. There are several more poetic feet but we will not go into them. If interested in them buy my *Little Booklets #15A and 15B,* available at the address below.

I write mostly in 4—4, a line of four beats followed by a line of four beats, or 4—3, four beats followed by three beats. Repeating the two lines gives you four lines called a Quatrain. I mostly write in quatrains. Another part of my Style or Voice is that I capitalize the first letter of each line, just something I do. I also use punctuation.

So now you know who I am, who I was. The contents of this book are poems I've written from November 2022 to now, November 2023. They are numbered in the ordered way they were written so don't look for a selected collection, just a look at how I felt during that year. I hope you find them enjoyable and maybe relatable to your life.

A last thought about my poems, you won't be left with a "What does he mean?" The poems are narrative, they tell a story— a beginning, middle and end.

Glen

Glen Wasson
2600 South 4th Avenue
Yuma, Arizona 85364
(928) 318-4306

iii

iv

Dedication

I dedicate this book

to my wife

Michelle

who has suffered through

hours of neglect

as I pursue my passion

of poetry.

Acknowledgment

A special acknowledgment

to a dear friend

and one time neighbor

Julia Christopher

for her continued support

and encouragement.

#629
But An Old Man

In body I am but an old man
But feel quite young in heart.
I have a smile, even a grin
Look forward to the day.

Already slept away half day
This COVID wears you down.
But have desires and wants to face
My life continues on.

My mind is happy all today
My mind is happy and gay.
Life has been good to me, I'd say
I've lived a long, long life.

Have no desire to see it end
Has been so good to me.
I have Michelle within my life
She makes my life complete.

This is my intro into book four
A simple little poem.
To say just how I feel today
The start of something new.

Glen Wasson
November 22, 2022

#630
All Mankind

How do we look into all mankind
To see what it is they have wroth?
Are we all up to see, the day that has passed
Or do we just wonder and think?

We know that mankind has struggled a while
We're not so new in times.
Billions have been and billions will be
Carry the travels that are.

Are we beyond what we were back then
Or are we stuck where we were?
Are we ahead, or are we behind
From where we started this walk?

We have much more, in a technical way
Computers and phones and planes.
Can talk around the world in time
But will our minds be able?

Perhaps our minds are a bit too slow
To keep up with what's been given.
Perhaps we must grow a direction to know
To understand just where we are.

This whole world that we now claim to know
With thoughts of knowledge and smarts
Do we really perceive what we think we know
Or are we just wasting away?

So proudly we stand at the edge of a cliff
Saying "Look at us straight and tall!"
Are we really at times when we understand
Or only a step from a fall?

Are we able to hold a style that we have
Or will we fail in the end?
Have we grown too big for the britches we wear
And taken too much for a goal?

Questions arise asking what do we know
About that which we seem to know.
So much before we came on the scene
So much will pass when we're gone.

How do we stand when compared with the rest
Are we there, or falling behind?
Will we as mankind continue to grow
Or have we crested the hill?

Is there more out there that we have to learn
Or have we learned it all?
Dare we to reach out, say more to be gained
Reach out and grab for a star.

A humble way may guide us tomorrow
Use the mind that's been given to us.
And temper it all with the heart that we have
Make proud those that came before.

Glen Wasson
November 25, 2022

#631
What Is The Goal

What is the goal of the people we are
Is it one we are able to reach?
Or is it beyond our tenuous grasp
Unable to reach our goal?

Life may never seem to be
Fair in all its ways.
Must all stand up for what we need
And settle for the rest.

We stand and look about the plain
Survey in all 360.
So much can come within our reach
Will it be worth the effort?

Life, what is this life we face
Worth it, or a waste?
A struggle that we all must face
Will not be all so easy.

We stand and wonder why it is
That we cannot complete?
From what the world has thrown at us
Perhaps we should rebel?

If life s not fair and we rebel
Who is to judge our effort?
Will it be fair, or biased still
Will justice ever be?

If this is all that life can give
If we must settle for this?
Who should say, "There's no more for you!"
No more that we can have.

Life's not worth it if it's all
That we can have today.
Turn into yourself, put your head in the sand
Turn your back unto the world.

Have we turned 360 round
From good, to bad, to good?
Perhaps we should take a good look around
Refresh our way of looking?

Look for the good that life has to give
Look up to the heavens above.
Look at the world from a new point of view
Start out on a brand new path.

Rejoice, be happy, smile again
A new life you have begun.
Step with a dance, float in the air
See wonders in your face.

Glen Wasson
November 26, 2022

#632
Another Little Poem

Another little poem to write
Another in my journal.
My mind keeps going on and on
Can't even turn it off.

Have been locked up for two weeks now
The CIVID bug has got us.
First me, then her, we both got it
Am trying to survive.

Don't like to be confined to room
Would rather be out free.
But rules are rules, I guess I'll be
The one who stays inside.

I drink my coffee, eat my meals
The daily ritual done.
Will sometime greet the outside air
Be good to feel the sun.

Soar throats and cough and all that stuff
Are part of what we have.
Don't seem to get too well too soon
We really feel the blahs.

Here's hoping we'll feel better soon
Enough of feeling lousy.
Just give us time when feeling good
And send us on our way.

Glen Wasson
November 27, 2022

#633
Off And On

The quarantine's off, the masks are on
We now may go outside.
This COVID crap don't like at all
Am glad that it's all over.

But still we cough, that still remains
Still do not feel the better.
And glad they say we're negative
Able to proceed.

Now able to go out—about
And see the other people.
Don't know how much you miss it so
Am glad to be about.

People are meant to be together
We're not meant to be alone.
We need to see another face
To smile and greet the one.

Glen Wasson
November 28, 2022

#635
Rainbow

Did you ever see a rainbow
When it wasn't nice outside?
The storm has passed, the rain is ore
Tis peaceful all about.

The rainbow stands for a promise kept
Was set so long ago.
No flood will envelope the earth again
Will never come again.

The bow it reaches high above
The ends, they touch the ground.
We may run over, seek the end
Yet never find the pot.

That pot of gold, so promised in lore
Just never seems to be
Right where was promised it to be
Tis always just beyond.

The bow is there for us to enjoy
And relish in Gods word.
He keeps His promise, yes He does
Another of His gifts.

So stand outside, lift up your eyes
And treasure this brief moment.
Will soon be gone, but will return
After a storm has passed.

Glen Wasson
November 30, 2022

#636
Swinging With Poetry

Swinging with poetry, yes I do
I swing both back and forth.
I like the rhythm as it flows
It's like a marching band.

I like the cadence and the meter
How it ebbs and flows.
Just like a gentle stream we see
It brings the peace to me.

Poetry exposes my whole body
My heart, my mind, my soul.
My very being I put forth
In hope that it will work.

Not always will the poem work out
Sometimes they cease to walk.
Sometimes they stumble and they trip
Is not a perfect beat.

But when time's right, the words they flow
With rhythm, beat and rhyme.
Create something to be proud of
And bring a smile to face.

Glen Wasson
November 30, 2022

#637
How To Write A Poem

This is the way to write a poem
Must get yourself in comfort.
Take your pen within your hand
And place it on the paper.

You move the pen both back and forth
And leave the marks behind.
These marks upon the paper are
The poem you meant to write.

So now you know how easily
A poem, it is to write.
Get out your pen and paper
Express yourself tonight.

Glen Wasson
December 1, 2022

#638
The Round Marble

The marble's round, the earth is too
Round, as round, as round.
There are no places flat or deep
The earth is simply round.

While some may hold to a flat earth thought
I must accept as round.
We've seen the pics sent from the moon
It certainly looks as round.

As little boys we often had
A pocket full of marbles.
We'd play at recess, noontime too
Would often play for keeps.

What keeps the oceans in their place
Why don't they just run out?
The places that we call "Down under"
What keeps them in their place?

I know that there is gravity
And that is how it works.
But still I like to wonder why
It doesn't fall apart?

I write this as a little boy
Who questions everything.
Will grow into a man someday
Accept what I am told.

But for a time I still will be
A little boy with marbles.
They're round and smooth and have a worth
They still feel good to me.

As grown-up must act adult
And do our jobs as told.
Get up, go work, go raise your kids
Teach them to be adults.

But for a little moment more
Just let them be a kid.
They soon enough take on the world
Forget about their marbles.

Glen Wasson
December 6, 2022

#639
The Pillow

When I lay my head on my pillow tonight
At the end of another day
My mind reviews events of the day
Reminds me of what I've done.

The softness envelopes my head a bit
It cushions the end of day.
Will be the place I'll spend the night
Recoup for the day to come.

What did I intend to do today
Did I finish or reach my goal?
Did I greet the day with a smile on my face
Did I leave it a better place?

Life's not always a happy place
It has its ups and downs.
We ebb and we flow with the time that we have
We really have little control.

Perhaps my mind will shut itself off
And let me rest and dream.
Renew my strength for the day to come
A day to wonder and think.

Will the new day bring joy and happiness
Or will it be doom and gloom?
Do I control my destiny
Or simply follow the crowd?

But for a time I still will be
A little boy with marbles.
They're round and smooth and have a worth
They still feel good to me.

As grown-up must act adult
And do our jobs as told.
Get up, go work, go raise your kids
Teach them to be adults.

But for a little moment more
Just let them be a kid.
They soon enough take on the world
Forget about their marbles.

Glen Wasson
December 6, 2022

#640
Dog On My Bed

There's a dog on my bed, laid out full length
Spread out all over the bed.
Would have to move...make room for me
He thinks he owns it all.

It is my fault, invited him in
To spend some time with me.
I think he loves me best of all
I am his favorite human.

As I look at the bed the dog is still there
Checking his world about.
Then lays his head back down to rest
And wait for another moment.

Sometimes I wish I were a dog
To live the life he lives.
To eat and sleep and take a walk
And feel the humans presence.

He's off the bed...has found his mom
I know, I have to share.
But he'll be back when he needs real love
I know he loves me more.

Glen Wasson
December 8, 2022

#641
My Desk

My desk is not against the wall
It sits before a window.
The blinds are closed, can't see outside
But still I see the light.

It's not too big, it's rather small
I oft run out of room.
It holds most of the things I need
Could always ask for more.

My computer and mouse are right up front
They are my main attraction.
The lamp's right there to shed its light
My journal to the right.

Across the back the speakers stand
They amplify the sound.
And in the back, don't take much room
They're simply just right there.

There is a drawer to hold small things
Though some might call it junk.
I am a poet, need those things
Cannot get rid of them.

I spend a lot of time right there
I sit, I think, I ponder.
With pen in hand I write it down
And later type it in.

My desk is needed much each day
To write and type my poetry.
It seems to be a pleasant place
It even holds my coffee.

Next to my desk there is a stand
Upon which sits my printer.
Below that ink and paper too
Required to share my poems.

The space is small in which it stands
It is my personal space.
I write, I type, I do produce
Within this little space.

If you're a writer, hope you have
Your very own personal desk.
To spend your own exciting time
Being quite productive.

Glen Wasson
December 10, 2022

#645
Beats

Anapest Tetrameter – two unstressed syllables & one stressed, four feet per line

Count the beats, count the beats, you must just count the beats
Clap them out if you need, clap them one two and three,
Put a break as it must at the end of the beats
Count the beats, count the beats, you must just count the beats.

And a poem's more than just words and lines on a page
It's a movement and sound and a little bit more.
An emotion and thought, heartfelt feelings and yet
It's a poem that's well written, that goes with the flow.

Like a poem that just steps out it marches and goes
Like a band that just marches it right down the street.
That's a poem as it flows with it's highs and it's lows
Does my mind think like that or just simply my heart?

As a dog running free at the end of it's leash
So a poem must be free here to find it's own place.
Searching here, searching there, searching most everywhere
Just to find its local in a world that is strange.

Let your poems flow as waters in midst of a stream
Let them ripple and turn as they follow the land.
Let them enter new land where they never have been
Let them burst on the world with a wizz and a bang.

When you scan poems, count beats, count the beats, not the words
Count them one two and three then you follow by beats.
With this new way of counting just try it and see
If it puts a new step in the way that you write?

When you use a new form in the way that you write
You will find that it might turn to be a delight.
It may twist and may turn in a way new to you
That is why we write poems in the way that we do.

Glen Wasson
December 13, 2022

#646
Love

What kind of love are we talking about
There are so many kinds.

There is the love God has for us
That is the highest kind.
He loves us with unending love
The kind that lives forever.

There is the love a mother has
For one and all her children.
A love that lasts a lifetime through
Goes on for generations.

A families love is deep and pure
It can be very wide.
It loves over here, it loves over there
It's love encompasses all.

The love between the neighbors
Is true in all its ways.
Through life and caring, continues on
Protects and looks out for.

In younger years there's puppy-love
A boy has for his girl.
Before he finds what real love is
It is his deepest love.

There is the love a teacher has
For each and all her students.
It's mostly in the lower grades
She sees them grow, mature.

Cannot forget the young adults
They have their time to love.
Beyond the puppy-love of kids
They know this love is true.

We all must grow, must all mature
To find an intimate love.
The love that makes the marriage bed
Will have to love a lifetime.

There's also love between two friends
This loves not like the others.
It's based on mutual care, respect
Survives long times apart.

Cannot forget the love we have
For all our pets and animals.
They look to us with eyes so true
We have to love them back.

I'm sure there's other kinds of love
This simple mind's forgot.
That's for a different time and place
To sit, to think, to write.

Glen Wasson
December 15, 2022

#647
Wi-Fi

What is this Wi-Fi we find so demanding
That we feel that we need all the time?
It's only been ten—twenty years at the most
That it's even been known of.

We have smart phones, appliances too
They all run off Wi-Fi.
Whether at home or a smart business place
We all seem to need Wi-Fi.

I'm sitting here now without Wi-Fi
The router must be down.
It is supplied by the office below
I am too needy to loose it.

It's back on now, I get to go!
Back to computer and just sign in.
Will not be back for quite a while
The Wi-Fi's on again.

Glen Wasson
December 15, 2022

#650
Writing A Poem

Again I'm sitting, writing here
To just renew my thoughts.
It's been a while since pen in hand
It's been a while for me.

Why must I write three poems today?
Why must I use my mind?
To think, arrange the words in line,
To fill my searching soul?

Writing a poem gives comfort to me
It brings me joy and peace.
And satisfaction, deep inside
Brings everything to be.

Why can't I take my life as it is
Why must I wish for more?
Must be the poet deep in me
Is always asking more.

Today I'll write, complete the poem
And add it to my list.
Add satisfaction to how I live
With that which fills my soul.

Glen Wasson
December 27, 2022

#651
My Own Strange Way

I write my poems in my own strange way
I do it to be different.
The rules I know I seem to break
The others I don't follow.

I like to twist the words around
They say it's not to be.
But I still like to be unique
What I call poetry.

I like my four line stanzas
I like feet four and three
I like the lines to march right on
I like the words to flow.

I use contractions quite a bit
I guess that's how I talk.
Perhaps I am a lazy one
It's just the way I am.

I like to tell a story
About some part of life.
I have a lot to write about
I've lived a long, long life.

I start each line with a capital
Some say that I should not.
That's how they did it way back when
That's how I do it now.
Sometimes I use a hook to end
A gotcha or a moral.
To let you see another side
Of what I've talked about.

We all could use a helping hand
To rise above our troubles.
To look at life another way
To ask another question.

We all must learn to stand up tall,
To put a smile on face.
To think of us as something good
To think we're doing better.

So think of something new today
Create a new persona.
The seeds been sown, now to grow
A time for you to bloom.

Glen Wasson
December 27, 2022

#652
Gone Are the Days

Gone are the days that try men's souls,
Those are the days that were.
No longer faced in the world today
No longer is the way.

There once were kings and kingdoms too
With castles strong and high.
Surrounded all around by moats
To keep the bad men out.

Within the castles were knights of old
With armor, shields and swords.
They all rode out to fight the wars
And woo all the fair maidens.

Fair maidens dwelt within the place,
They graced the tables daily.
They danced and did what maidens did,
And lovely ones they were.

To bring them joy and happiness
They had a jester too.
To dance and play the flute and lyre
And tell the funny stories.

To make all this run smooth and right
There were a lot of servants.
They did the work that had to be
They were the ones that worked.

So now you know how castles were,
Who sat and ate and played,
And also who it was that did
The work that needed done.

Glen Wasson
December 27, 2022

#653
Here We Are All
Sailing

So here we are all sailing round, somewhere out here in space.
A tilted axis world we ride and circle round the sun.

The spin gives us our day and night, the tilt provides the seasons.
The star, our sun, gives us our light, each circle adds a year.

Around our earth we have a moon, and round and round it goes.
It shines on us reflected light but looks on us in parts.

The moon goes round the earth in time but doesn't have an axis.
It doesn't spin, just goes around, the face is all we see.

I wonder how it'll all work out; the sun, the earth, the moon?
Will always be around this way or will it fail someday?

Am I so smart I've figured it out, or do I brag too much?
I'll leave it up to you to say, it's more than I can do.

Glen Wasson
December 27, 2022

#654
New Years Eve
2022-23

The old is winding down right now
The year is almost done.
What have we done to improve this world
Will they even know we've been?

There are wars and problems everywhere
Migration is now world wide.
People are fleeing the problems they face
To go to a questioning place.

Tonight there are fireworks and party's to go
Tomorrow they'll be feasting with joy.
Most of us hope the new will be good
But many will question that.

What does a new year mean to us now?
Why do we even wonder?
Tuesday will be a workday again
Wednesday, it'll all be over.

Okay, New Year, show us your best
Lead us to something high!
Help us to relish everything new
Be open to all you bring.

Glen Wasson
December 31, 2022

#655
Change

What would it be if we all liked the same, if we all liked the very
    same thing?
Like is a sort of, a preference, for me, going on in a way that I like.
That is just some of the things that we do, that we do just to be
    what we are.
Now is the time that we stand up and say, this whole thing is an
    ugly old thing.

People are funny in what they will do, what we'll do in our own
    stupid way.
We are the ones that are needing it all, being needy and greedy and
    all.
Would we all change in a bettering way if we only had guts to be
    there?
That would be something that could come to be, that would be for
    the best of us all.

What would I like, be the best for myself, would to be something
      better than me.
Better is better than nothing at all, be it good, be it bad, be it not.
I would be better if only I would try to change the way that I
      change me.
Try to be better in some simple way, simply one little way if I
      could.

If I could change you, I really would change, what you are, when
      you do, what you do.
You are the reason I am what I am, can't be fault of a man such as I.
I wont change, you must change, you must all change-- right
      now no desire to change me.
This is the reason I've written all this, if only would change how I
      feel.

Sorry if this is the end of this poem, it's the end of my efforts till
      now.
Maybe I'll learn to be open and grow--sometime I'll grow and
      learn.
This is the end of this curious rant, be it this or be that, be it
      nothing.
Better be this than be nothing at all, be the end of the things in my
      mind.

Glen Wasson
January 1, 2023

#656
Walking The Dog

Tonight Michelle and I we walked the dog
It must be done quite often to be sure.
The name he answers to is Bucky dog
He does well on a leash when we take care.

He pulls hard though we think we're in control
And walks a bit more faster than we do.
We follow him about at end of leash
Seems like he is the leader of us all.

To be a sled-dog he would do so well.
He pulls hard and is leader of the pack,
Until he catches scent of something else
And takes off in direction of his own.

So that's the story of our dog named Bucky,
A dog that I write poems about today.
He's more a family member than a pet,
We love him with a love that will not end.

Glen Wasson
January 6, 2023

#657
Glider

I sit here in the glider seat, gliding back and forth,
Listening to the melody, of the babbling brook.
Resting in the light there is, of the brilliant sun.
What a way to spend the day, a day without a care.

Some people though, they sweat and strain, working at a job.
Others still they lay around and never give a darn.
Some will work at jobs they hate, are doomed to never change.
Why the difference in these groups, why aren't they all the same?

Some have jobs and some have none though life does not seem fair.
Just the way the dice are rolled, life's just a game of chance.
Be the one who changes things things and rolls the dice again,
Take the life that's given you and make the best of it.

Smile and let your face shine through, never have a frown,
Show the world your better than the ones you left behind.
No time for you to be depressed or have a pity party.
Now you are a new creature and always looking up.

Glen Wasson
January 7, 2023

#658
A Pile of Change

A pile of change lays on my desk
The contents of my pocket.
It took me several days to get
It all accumulated.

I notice some are old and dull
And others new and shinny.
And yet they're worth the same amount
Does not decrease their value.

Dimes are the smallest of the coins
Then pennies and the nickles.
Quarters we see often now
The halves not all that much.

Now these are all American coins
Don't know about the others.
And yet they work most everywhere
At least I think they do.

In the past I also had
A case or ring of keys;
The house, the car, the trunk and gas.
I used to have a lot.

So now I'm down to one or two
Don't have so much to lock.
When I was rich I had lots more
To secure with many locks.

So now I'm down to one or two
Don't have so much to lock.
When I was rich I had lots more
To secure with many locks.

As a retired senior one,
I have so little now.
Thieves don't bother me much now
Don't want what I possess.

I live within a gated place,
No uninvited guests
Or door to door to call on me,
I always sit in peace.

So that is why I write my poems
I've nothing else to do.
I sleep and eat and watch T.V.
And write my poetry.

To all of you who live real lives
Of family, kids and jobs.
Someday you too will reach my age
So find something to do.

Glen Wasson
January 9, 2023

#659
Cold Selling

There's a chill in the air, some might say it's a cold,
Too cold for a sweater, too warm for a coat.
Don't have a good answer, I couldn't say why,
The way that it is now will dictate the day.

Dare I sit on the glider and glide back and forth
Or sit on the bench, the cold concrete and all?
I think on the glider, poems come to my mind
They speak of the cold or will pass from my mind.

These are the words that I share with my friends
Words that are destined to fill my next book.
Hopefully someone will buy it to read
And share with their friends how they found it to read.

Do books sell in weather as cold as today
Or wait for the Spring when it's warm with blue sky?
A poet does not get his money from books
A day job is needed to pay all his bills.

Is this the new way that I advertise mine
To stand reading poems with my hat on the ground
Or going on air if a station will do?
How do I get my books in front of you?

Am out of my comfort don't know what to do
To go out and market these books that I wrote?
I'm proud of them surely they came from my heart
The words that I write are all I have left.

Glen Wasson
January 17, 2023

#660
Life in General

Life in general, what is it like
Is it just what we do or also our thoughts?
Are our lives so complex, can't define who we are?
Do our thoughts and our deeds combine while we're here?

Thoughts and deeds, just what does that mean?
Is it something that's real or something that's remote?
The pen, it is real and the paper is too,
Do we live in the present, is there even a past?

Am I making too much of the thoughts that I have
Are things really diverse as I make them to be?
Can there be something simple to put it to rest
Must I suffer in wonder while waiting the word?

This all is beyond me, I don't want to know
If I'm coming or going at such a fast pace?
Will I ever find out what the truth is to me?
Must I sacrifice all just to know what it means?

Life is all clothed in these questions and more
Than a simple mind dares to attempt to take in.
Coming and going, perhaps all around,
Which is the right one for humans to go?

Dare we pursue what we don't understand?
Pick another direction and go in that way
Or drunkenly stumble off walls on both sides
Tell me please, tell me please, what's the way I should go?

Life is confusing for minds such as mine
Simple in thought and desiring to know
Is it even within the tight grasp of my hand
To seek after things like the fabled brass ring.

Oh, how I wish things would simply clear up
The waters be stilled and the clouds disappear?
Sunlight and stars become now so distinct
Moonlight to give us a gentle nights sleep.

I want to slow down and just glide back and forth
Let my mind float in a field yet unknown.
Release the world to become what it must
Free of restraints I once held it to.

Let go and release and no longer hold on
To a world that is held to a greater restraint.
Let it flow to a tune that it always has heard
Let it go, let it go, let it go, let it go.

Glen Wasson
January 22, 2023

#661
The Day is Cool

The day is cool but not too cold
The wind is barely blowing.
The sky's so blue it seems unreal
Another day in Yuma.

The town I live in is sort of big
About one hundred thou.
Not big if you're the city folk
But makes an easy fit.

I've had my breakfast, walked the dog
Returned and watched a class.
And now I've taken pen in hand
To write a simple poem.

Michelle is in the other room
The other one of two.
She plays her games and finds her words
She is my other half.

Bucky's the dog that lives with us
He saunters back and forth
To visit one and then the other.
He makes it all his own.

Lunchtime will come in a little while
I'll get my coat and walk
Into the dining-room to eat
And join my table mates.

The afternoon will venture on
Will need to find a way
To spend my time productively
And not to simply age.

Life goes on at Y.S.L.
A simple schedule rules,
Seven, twelve and four PM
Are only what we need.

The rest is up to us to do
To entertain ourselves.
Though bingo, crafts and other things
Provide something to do.

As senior people we don't have
A job or other things,
Requiring us to discipline
Our time as in the past.

So we continue, day by day
To eat and sleep in leisure.
Our waking time is ours to spend
In any way we wish.

So life is what we make it
Some good, some bad, some blah.
It's ours to spend just as we please
I hope we spend it well.

Glen Wasson
January 25, 2023

#662
A Place To Rest My Hand

Iambic Heptameter

This journal is the place where I can rest my weary hand
And place it on the empty page awaiting my first stroke.
The pen I hold within that hand is loaded up with ink
The time has come for ink to flow on down unto the sheet.

Will words make sense as they form down there on the empty page
Or will I have to find a better way to say my thoughts?
These lines are long and difficult to write up to the end
The stanza's full of many words that I have had to think.

Have picked a meter that is not an easy one to write
Has seven beats in every line that falls upon the page.
The first is soft and lightly said, the accent's on the next
Continues on throughout the line until the end is reached.

Am happy with the challenge that I've placed upon myself
It makes me work and wiggle some to make it all work out.
And some would say I'm sort of dumb to make this job so hard
I think I'm up to doing it, will give it a good try..

I think that this is going well and I will soon succeed
Beginning to sustain the beat I'm feeling in my head.
I'm counting beats, I'm feeling beats, their coming to me now
I can't stop now, I must go on and write a few more lines.

I think I'm proud, my ego's up, my head is getting big
Who else would try this course of action just to prove a point.
Okay, that's all that I will do at this here time in time
Will go review what I have done and see if I've done well.

Glen wasson
January 27, 2023

#663
The Air is Brisk

Iambic Pentameter

The air is brisk but still unlike the night
The time is telling, dawn is soon to be.
No one's about, they're still at rest in bed
The day's not here, we still would call it night.

But in the east the dawn begins to glow
Not visible except to those who know.
The wildlife soon will rise and start to roam
The glow will soon become a bright sunrise.

Dark shadows still fill up the distant east
But fast the light is coming into sight.
Soon everything will welcome in the morn
A day has come as night begins to fade.

No more will darkness swallow up the earth
With light the dwellers go about their lives.
Along with lives that we know nothing of
A day is moving forth with all its might.

Though daylight beings go about their lives
Night-time ones are deeply in their rest.
As if the two will never, ever meet
Because they habitat two different planes.

This makes for something different for us all
As if two worlds exist in the same place.
We only have a thought about the other
Perhaps that's all we'll ever need to know.

Glen Wasson
January 28, 2023

#664
So Hard to Write

So hard to write when words don't come,
So hard to force them out.
Now need to look so far inside
To find what is not there.

Would be so nice if words would come
And flow as free as water
And never stop behind a dam
To stifle all your thoughts.

A brick wall seems to be my goal
Cannot see something better.
To beat my head against again
Like has been done before.

Have seen those days before in time
Though not so very often.
Would like for them to leave me now
And let me rest in peace.

I've found a word, now three or four
The faucet drips a bit.
Will not supply a thirsty man
But will prevent a death.

A poet struggles for the word
Not any word, but one.
The very best to put in place
To balance out the line.

A line must flow, must have a beat
To match up with the next.
A crack could cause a toe to stub
And stumble on its way.

Now words are flowing once again
The lines are adding up.
Now several stanzas have appeared
To grace the page their on.

A poem is forming as I write
It's coming into life.
Will need to bear the pain of birth
And learn to breath alone.

They do not come along at ease
Sometimes must be induced.
When waiting for the words to come
No longer seems to do.

This one started out that way
Was pushing all uphill.
But finely found a level place
The work began to ease.

Take time, rejoice and stand up free
A new poem has been birthed.
Has seen the light of day for once,
Will see if it survives.

Glen Wasson
January 31, 2023

#665
The Words Within

The mind has loosed the words within
The stream's begun to flow.
Cannot restrain the waters cold
Must loose them into nature.

The Earth that circles, spins and tilts
Accepts the flow described
Replenishes all around the globe,
These words are being freed.

Maybe in print or on the net
I will release them all,
to be received and read aloud
And thought and pondered too.

This little poem is short and sweet
Will not take long to read,
But will contain a thought or two
To challenge one to think.

Go forth dear words, go forth and spread
Your wings onto the wind.
Be free of all restraints that bind
Arise unto the sun!

Glen Wasson
January 31, 2023

#666
Cloudy Skies

After a day of cloudy skies the sun has just appeared,
Must be below the clouds that were way up there in the sky.
Why do we miss the sun that shines between the morn and night?
How can we not just sit and wait until it turns out right?

Down here in Yuma town we like to see the sun each day
We miss it when it doesn't shine and brighten up our day.
It helps the crops to grow, produce, provide the leafy greens
That flood the markets all around the mighty U.S.A.

It now is dark, the sun has set, no more the sun will shine
It seems to happen every day at just about this time.
Good thing that it's consistently that way around the clock
Will have to wait for day to come and bring back the old sol.

Glen Wasson
February 5, 2023

#667
The Wind

The wind blows across the field
and the wheat

        waves

              and

                          waves.

I sit under a tree and hear
the leaves rustle overhead.

Looking up I see the leaves bobbing to and fro.

The wind is warm and touches my face
but its sound is hardly heard.

Glen Wasson
February 4, 2023

#669
A Poem of Couplets

I went to the door, the sky was blue
I opened the door and cried out "Sue!"

She hollered back, "What are you doing?"
"Nothing really, just pursuing."

Life is rough out where I live
I want to take but only give.

Some days it looks like it will rain
Those are days I feel the pain.

I'm on my own, I have a car
but Mom, she tells me, "Don't go far."

I should have done this yesterday
but since I didn't now I'll pay.

Poetry comes naturally
that is why they come to me.

Why do you stand and look at me
I often wonder what you see.

Why do you type in all those words
when in the end we'll eat some curds.

This is the end of this here poem
now's the time to laugh and moan.

Glen Wasson
February 4, 2023

#670
Going to Lunch

Was going to lunch at noon today
I did not bring my jacket.
The sun was warm upon my back
And then I spied the glider.

It sat with open skies above
And not a bit of shade
I knew I'd have to rest awhile
Enjoy this sacred spot.

I sat me down to glide a bit
I went both back and forth.
I closed my eyes to quiet me
Became just me alone.

I slowly glided back and forth
Was such a gentle feeling.
The sun it blessed my open side
I welcomed it to me.

I glided in the seat I sat
Enjoyed it oh so much.
I turned off all the outside world
And simply looked within.

Wish everyone could find a place
With glider or a swing.
They bring a comfort seldom felt
Within a busy day.

Glen Wasson
January 31, 2023

#673
To Lead a Class

I lead a class in poetry
Tis something I enjoy.
I spend a lot of time to get
The handouts that I give.

I try to share the love I have
The love that's still quite new
To give them reason to go on
And learn a little more.

It's not a job when it's love you share
You lead it from the heart,
To pass it on to those who hear
Encourage them to grow.

They seem to be ashamed to share
Their thoughts upon a page
I give them words and prompts and such
To lead them it to write.

It's great to see their eyes light up
When something strikes their fancy.
They talk, discuss between themselves
As if I am not there.

What would I do with a Saturday morn
If I didn't lead the group?
Would likely be on internet
To see what I could find.

We meet and greet and sit around
The room of 233.
It's warm and pleasant, comfortable
And also free to use.

This public space holds several things
But ours, we use it well.
We listen to a poem or two
May study how it's made.

But now we struggle to write it down
I question how to lead.
May have to take them by the hand
And guide them word by word.

So choose a word to fill the blank
You choose from three or four
And in the end you have a poem
Take home and let it dwell.

Glen Wasson
February 8, 2023

#674
War is Hell

Don't want to go to hell right now, I want to go to heaven
It seems so much the better place, I think I would prefer.
But what would God say when I'm there, would He accept me in?

Now I've said it, cast my lot, into this terrible plot
I've dug a hole, I can't get out I must accept my place.
No one but me to walk this path, I'll have to walk alone.

There is no joy within my heart I'm really feeling bad
How can I resurrect myself from what I've done to me?
Clean up my act and purify and sanitize my life.

It's up to me, nobody else, to fight this all alone
Take up my sword and sharpen it and ride on into war.
I have a horse, a shield and sword and now I need my wits.

Will I survive this frightful place or will I need more nerve?
Can taste the blood and feel the fear abiding all about.
When will it end, will I survive or will I taste of death?

I fight with all the strength I have but it is drawing near
I'm on the ground and rolling round, is this to be my end?
My open eyes belie my place, I find myself in bed.

Glen Wasson
February 8, 2023

#675
Looking Through a Window – 2023

I'm looking through a window
I'm looking in, not out.
I see what is a family place
A family place, a home.

A family with a mom and dad
A family with some kids.
You add them up, they make a bunch
Encased in love and space.

Here is a room that is so warm
Compared to what's outside.
A fire is lit within the hearth
The family cat rests there.

They do not feel the snow that falls
They never fear the cold.
A comfort fills the room they're in
A family lives within.

Glen Wasson
February 13, 2023

#676
Where I Am From
– 2023

Small towns
German pancakes
Sour cream cookies
Strawberry shortcake with biscuits

First years of life
Nebraska schools
First and second grades'
WWII and shortages
All by the time I'm seven

'39 Chevy, '40 Mercury
Traded cars for tires
Sunburn summers
Goldfish ponds
Stubbed toes that bled

Moved four times
Sent back to third
Long division
Third state
Picked hops for pay

Now I'm ten
Moved two more times
Back to my home state
Nebraska

Cub Scouts, Boy Scouts
Setting pens and selling Grit
Moved three more times
Graduated and moved

Basic training, trainee job
Bought a car younger than me
Worked two years and moved again
Entered my fifth state

Turned twenty-one
Went to college
Quit mid term
Moved and got a job

Changed jobs and moved
Another state
More jobs
More moves

Got married
Bought a house
Had a son
More jobs, more moves

Laid off and moved
Another son
Got job and moved
Heard from God

Quit job and moved
To another state
Began classes
Moved, moved, moved

Deputation, Africa
Birthed a daughter
Went back home

Got a job
A business
Found a new direction
Moved and found a job

Two more jobs
Five years
Laid off
Moved to new state

New job
New home
New church
Ten years

Divorced
Moved
New state
New job

Internet love
New wife
New house
New state

Lottery
One million
New car
Cruise

Retire
Find literature and books
Find poetry
Wife sick
Wife dies

New move
New life
New love
New wife

Now eighty-three
Twenty-three years in town
Feel permanent
Feel blessed

Glen Wasson
February 13, 2023

New job
New home
New church
Ten years

Divorced
Moved
New state
New job

Internet love
New wife
New house
New state

Lottery
One million
New car
Cruise

Retire
Find literature and books
Find poetry
Wife sick
Wife dies

New move
New life
New love
New wife

Now eighty-three
Twenty-three years in town
Feel permanent
Feel blessed

Glen Wasson
February 13, 2023

#677
A Bottle

A bottle lies upon the sand
A cork is in its mouth.
A paper rests inside the glass
What do we make of this?

Was just a walk upon the beach
A brightly, sunlit day.
The warmth inviting leisurely
To venture out alone.

A sight like this is new to me
Has never been before.
I bend to pick the bottle up
It now rests in my hand.

Adventure runs throughout my veins
Excitement through and through.
Begin to tremble where I'm at
I suddenly feel cold.

From where has this strange object come,
From near or very far,
From recently or long ago?
It smells of salty air.

I look around, I am alone
No others have observed
Me picking up this bottle here
And turning it about.

My curiosity takes hold of me
I wonder what's within?
Could be from generations past
Or only yesterday.

There seems to be some writing there
Upon the sheet within.
Will it be English or will it be
Some long forgotten tongue.

At first I want to open it
Pull out the paper sheet.
But that would end the mystery
Of what is there inside.

Is someone shipwrecked on an isl
In desperate need of help?
Or simply just a kid at play
To see where it would go.

I know that I must open it
To know the reason why
But that will then share everything
Expose it to the air.

With apprehension I reach for
The cork that seals the neck
I touch—it feels so dry and old
Perhaps I should not pull.

A quandary now envelops me
Do I really want to know?
Or take it home, a mystery
And place it on a shelf.

Could I stand it if I did
The contents left unread
And wonder as I pass it by
As I resume my life?

Again I reach to pull the cork
To satisfy my mind.
Open it, pull out the slip
And read what's written on.

That may be just what I must do
I must read what's inside.
Expose it to the world I'm in
And bring it all to life.

Yes I'll do it, pull the cork
And slip the paper out.
Unroll it after days of rest
And see what its about.

But wait, what happens if I do
Will I be any smarter,
Reading what somebody wrote
Sometime back there in time?

How long can I stay wondering
About this thing I have?
Can I contain my curious side
And simply let it be?

Or falter at some latter date
Remove the cork and read
What plainly is within the glass
And let my heart release.

A sigh, a sob, I know not what
Will come from deep within?
Emotion swells, can I contain
Or will it all drain out?

OK, I will, I'll open it
I'll open it today.
I pull the cork, it gives a pop
I sniff the air within.

I tilt the bottle, paper slides
I touch it with my finger.
I pull it down a little more
There, I have it out!

*"I need no help though I am on
a floating ball in space.
I'm living life as best I can
Hope you are doing well."*

Glen Wasson
February 14, 2023

#678
Tonight

Tonight I went to walk the dog
It's very cold and windy.
Bucky pulled hard on the leash
I think he felt the cold.

At my desk I hear the wind
It makes a funny sound.
Is more a rattle than a roar
I used to hear a whistle.

Throughout the night the wind kept up
It even rained a bit.
The seats were wet where the dogs can run
I had to stand and wait.

These sounds are not so common here
Don't always get the storms.
But when they come it's worth a write
Record them down in time.

Glen Wasson
February 14, 2023

#679
Where I Live

I write about the simple place I live
I don't get out that much to see the world.

I live two rooms, a bath, a wife, a dog
And eat my meals down in the dining room.

I do look out the front door and I see
I see the courtyard, orange trees, fountain too.

Am on the second floor so overlook
A balcony to see the world that's mine.

I'm writing at my desk in my bedroom
Sitting on the chair I take my rest.

My desk, it faces the window in front
And blinds prevent my eyes from looking out.

My laptop occupies the center stage
The lamp, it sets aside and to the left.

I either write about what is outside
Or what I reckon from my simple mind.

So now you know from what it is I write
You know about as much as even I.

Glen Wasson
February 17, 2023

#680
Is, Was and Will Be

Is is today, Was is yesterday and Will Be is tomorrow

We live in a time that always passes
Time that Is and Was,
The Will Be isn't here right now
But Will Be will be Is.

We exist on a spot in time
A spot that we call Is.
However Is will be a Was
When tomorrow comes around.

Today was tomorrow yesterday
What Is was Will Be then.
Every step we take in the pace of time
Is Is which is now a Was.

Time is like a river full
Of water ever flowing.
Upstream are days of Will Be
Downstream are days of Was.

Is is an instant, a spot in time
A spot of Will Be to us.
But Is is the Will Be that was to be
And is now that spot in time.

This poem is not the same it was
Back when I started writing.
It's passing from Is to Was, a past
Never to come again.

Is time as hard as I make it to be
Like riding a merry-go-round?
Seeing Will Be and Is and Was
Dare we step off and claim a bit of Is?

Best we can live in the Is that is
And make the best of it.
The past is gone, can't change again
Today is all we've got.

Today we can change what we're doing today
Can change for the better to be
And look for the Will Be tomorrow will bring
Another chance to change.

If you stand in the bed of a flowing stream
And look up above, it's clear.
But looking down we see the cloudy
Water we've stirred up.

Are we ever really in control
Can we ever change for good?
It seems we're on a slippery slope
And destined to fall down.

Look up, take hold of God's hand
Take hold, He'll lift you up
And even if you don't believe
It still is worth a try.

Glen Wasson
February 18, 2023

#681
Life

Life is like—so often said
Sometimes beyond what we describe.
It starts—it stops, but in between
It is what we call life.

Sometimes I stand, sometimes I sit
But always leads to wonder.
What would be if we knew more
So would it help or hinder?

I visualize a merry-go-round
But really a railway.
It's round and round but never the same
It's always never ending.

I gaze into the western air
As I sit upon my chair.
I see two dots of light up there
And wonder—do I care?

I know that they're not stars I see
They're planets cause they move.
They're Jupiter and Venus too
Carousing round our sun.

Such is life without a goal
Just circling our sun.
Yet never getting anywhere
Just keeping, going round.

The merry-go-round is dizzying me
A little sickening too.
The railway gives adventure though
And leads you to relax.

Each station is always new to me
It makes me wonder how
Would be to get off, start anew
And see where it would go?

The train has started, too late now
An option now gone past.
Will never come to me again
My life continues on.

So round and round and on and on
Such is life to me.
At this little, dinky, spot in time
Along eternity.

Will have to live the life I have
Will not be given other.
It's up to me what I will choose
No one can do for me.

Glen Wasson
February 20, 2023

#682
The Sky and Life

The sky is mostly blue today
But clouds are overhead.
It's chilly, not too cold today
But still not comfortable.

Would like it warmer, that'd be nice
To feel the sun on me.
It's pleasant just to take a pause
And let the world go by.

I'm presently in morning time
Had breakfast, wait for lunch.
Such is life when you're retired
Not really much to do.

Have walked the dog, made wife her coffee
Have one poem done and starting two.
Don't really want that much to do
That's why I'm where I'm at.

Have put my time in working hard
From forty hours to eighty.
Commuted sixty miles each way
Though sometimes just a mile.

So how do you face life today
Working hard or easy?
Hot outdoors or cool inside
I guess it just depends?

Retirement suits me well right now
Am happy where I'm at.
Three hots, a cot and a wife that loves
What more could I ask for?

I know that life is more than that
It's meant to have more meaning.
But I'll live mine and you live yours
And happy we will be.

At eighty three, will soon be four
I've lived a lot of life.
I've really had but few regrets
I'm pretty satisfied.

What more could I demand from life
Have lived a long, full life.
Would wish that every other one
Could be as pleased as I.

So here's to life, was good to me
I hope it will continue.
Enjoying what I have right now
And wish the best to you.

Glen Wasson
February 20, 2023

#683
Living

We're living in the here and now
There really is no other.
If we died now, there'd be no more
We'd only have the past.

What did we do last week, last month
That means so much to us?
Actions now are in the bank
That's all remains of us.

The life we live, both good and bad
Is what they will remember.
What is it we've contributed
In the whole scheme of the morrow?

We eat and sleep and move around
Some work, some play, some waste.
Our life is time, it's all we have
Consider how you spend.

Our life is but a spot in time
Eternity, the whole.
Billions have passed and billions will come
Few left a legacy.

Perhaps a few will notice me
And some may then remember.
What it was like back in our day
And how we made our lives.

How will they remember me
And random thoughts of you?
In the greater scheme of life,
The whole of all that is.

Not all of us can be real great
But all of us can be,
Can be the very best we can
And care for someone else.

Be kind and care, be gentle too
Greet people with a smile.
For some, that may be all they have
For them, will be enough.

For each of us, a legacy
We leave for all to see.
Some are great and some are small
For some, they gave their all.

Glen Wasson
February 21, 2023

#684
So Little Time

So much to say, so little time
My life is growing short.
They say we grow too old too soon
And that's just what it is.

Some will be an introvert
And not say very much.
Others can't be still at all
Yet nothing much to say.

It would be nice if words were great
But words don't rise above.
They may be good, they may be bad
They may be in-between.

We all believe that we are right
That we are just so smart.
And have wise words to freely share
With all the world around.

But that would make a poet be
That's one with words to share.
Can't hold them in, they must come out
They're now all yours to read.

Glen Wasson
February 21, 2023

#685
The Winds Emotion

The sight, the sound, the feeling of
The wind that blows today.
Outside I see and feel the wind
And hear it blow things round.

And inside as I sit at desk
The blinds, they slowly move.
The window doesn't close too tight
The filtered wind comes in.

The sound is very strange to me,
Sometimes a cart on wheels
It passes in the parking lot.
Sometimes, a simple whoosh.

It's gusty, blustery, violent too
So much is brought to life.
The wind's alive as anything
It seems to rule the scene.

It's sunny, should be warm outside
But cold it really is.
A heavy coat would be 'bout right
It sounds so nasty there.

Have been outside and felt the sting
Upon my face, my cheeks.
To see the trees, their leaves blown round
And taste the dust in air.

The room seems cold, although it's warm
It's what the wind has done.
No fun to be outside today
Much better, stay inside.

The wind, it moans and groans and sighs
Is not a pleasant sight.
It sends a harshness over you
Seems more like March than Feb.

I'm sure it'd pull a kite apart
This wind that shakes my being.
The window shakes and rattles too
Has gone the whole night through.

When will it end, this winter storm
When will it cease to blow?
When will the warmth return to us
When—when—when.

I've had about enough right now
I'm ready for an end.
To stop, quit, end it all
I've had enough for now.

Two pages I have used to write
About the wind today.
It can't go on for much more time
I simply wont allow.

What power do I have, you say
Command the wind to stop?
I have the sole desire within
A wish to see it end.

Throughout the day the wind repeats
The study scourge it is.
For hour after hour here
Right here in Yuma town.

Up North the Interstate is closed
The snow is piling up.
Trees are down, roads are closed
They have no school today.

I hear the window rattle
I see the blind blow in.
I feel a crispness in the air
I'm glad that I'm in here.

I'm not the only one to feel
This storm should just move on
And leave us all alone again
Await a better day.

Who really wants to live like this
I really want it better.
A calmer day to see tomorrow
And have our life returned.

Glen Wasson
February 22, 2023

#687
The Blinds

I sit at my desk and look into the blinds
The window is closed to the outside world.
I see but the slats of the blinds, full width
A few slats of light shine through.

Is this how I see the world before me,
Blind to what's clear to them?
Have I shut myself off from the life others see
Have I ceased to see life as it is?

Life is true, whatever it is
We only look at one view.
Do we look at life as a window or mirror
Looking out or only reflected?

Reflection is only the life that we view
If we give up the clearness of glass.
It is best that we take in the view that's out there
To see life as it really is.

Too often we close our eyes to what's out there
The world that plainly exists.
Should we ban all the books that are written about
The world we deny that's out there?

It's not new to us or our generation
It's happened so often before.
Mankind is afraid of a challenging word
Afraid to open our eyes.

Why do we feel we are masters of all
Denying all-others their view?
We're given a mind to investigate all,
What is this, what is that, what is life?

Perhaps this whole life is beyond what we see,
We only see what's out front?
To the side and the back is unknown to us
We only observe the half.

Why do others see what we don't,
Why don't we all agree?
Agree that the world is a flat screen ahead
Is only what we observe.

It hurts when we realize we only see half
Half of what is really out there.
Our ego's so large that we fully contain
All knowledge, all that is out there.

What about others, they also have minds
All others and many they be.
Are looking around in a way that we're not
And seeing what's out of our view.

We finally find out that our view is not all
Not all that is out there to see.
Be thankful that others are willing to share
What our limited vision can't see.

Glen Wasson
February 26, 2023

#688
Offended

The buzz-word today is "Offended."
Offended by this, offended by that.
Someone did something and I'm offended.
Someone said something, I am...

The skin of some people is very thin.
Can't take anything that offends.
And much of the world is offensive to them
They don't like it when they are offended.

For those offended I say "So what"
Go to your safe place and pout.
Go to a dark place and cover your ears,
Go, cause your feelings are hurt.

The world isn't made to cater to you
The world doesn't have to be fair.
Your feelings are not of any concern,
Most people don't care about you.

Shut up and come out of your shell of life
If you're an adult, grow up.
Stand up and don't cry yourself into a fit
Your worries are not my concern.

Hope this offends some fragile heart
Hope they will shed some tears.
Hope they will grow up and stand on their feet
And leave the world to be.

Glen Wasson
February 27, 2023

#689
Without Words

Without words to a poem what do we do?
I've only pen and paper in my hand.
My mind is blank without a single thought
Why do I even try to write a poem?

The net is slow, can't keep up with the show.
This paper wasted as the ink that flows.
I bragged about always having a start
But now my mind is empty as the air.

And yet I write these words upon the page
Will have to wait a while to feel them work.
No nature comes to greet the missing mind
No bit of life will reach out to be help.

To struggle as I do is not a joy
To throw the pen in utter madness down.
It's not my mind but still I want to write
Is this a devils mind that I have found?

A blackness has o'er-come the light that way
Have not a candle here to light a room.
Why must I write when all is lost to me?
The words just flow although I wish they'd stop.

Have paused a bit and ate and drank a beer
Body filled but mind is still empty.
Sundown here, light going, night is near
Will cease to write and end it all right here.

Glen Wasson
March 3, 2023

#690
Monday

An unfamiliar meter, Iambic hexameter

The sky is blue but not as blue as it could be,
There's clouds up there not often seen in Yuma town.
My breakfast's done, the dog is walked, the morning's on
The day's begun, what will it bring to make it full?

Have read the paper through and through, what is there left?
My lunch will come and dinner too, that much I know.
What will the afternoon bring now to make it all?
Complete with all that we desire, it is today.

The day continues as it goes so much will come.
We can not stop the travel of the sun, not now.
Must simply let it be and see what will it be.
We have no strength to order things, the power's gone.

In time the end will come and take away the day.
The light will fade when evening comes, the day will end.
A quiet sleep will overcome the day is gone.
Some rest and dreams will be our course until new day.

Glen Wasson
March 6, 2023

#691
Books

Book banning!

What are we saying about writing books
Does the one who is writing have life of his own?
If he does should he ride as a king over all?
Should his life over-rule all the words that he wrote?

Each one has a life and a writer no less
Some are good, even grand, all while others are bad.
Writers are human, though now some are not
Computers with chips often clash with the real.

Consider the source or see only results
A mechanical writer is not even real.
Could ten monkeys with keyboards maybe do the same?
Seen monkeys do awful while visiting the zoo.

So how do we look at the writer himself
Do we give him a pass if he dallies a bit?
Or hang him from yardarms as some would suggest
And burn all the books that he wrote in his life?

Glen Wasson
March 6, 2023

#692
Tuesday

The sky is gray, no blue today
The sun is hidden away.
The overcast subdues it all,
Slowly it appears.

It's almost warm, not cool today
A jacket's all required.
My major job, to walk the dog
Is done and I'm complete.

I got up early, had my meal,
Enjoy the morn that is.
Retirement—easy life to live
Not much you have to do.

Painting at ten, library at noon
My day is filling up.
Online learning, for a while
Back to the routine.

Will have to learn to rest a while
How to take it easy.
Wait for tomorrow, see what it brings
Don't want to be surprised.

Glen Wasson
March 7, 2023

#693
Evening

It's after five, it's evening time
The sun is in the west.
The sky's still blue with fluffy clouds
But will be passing soon.

Dinner's done, completed it
Now settle down to rest,
And let the quiet time take o'er
And wait for night to come.

A peaceful time of day it is
The cares are gone for now.
Too early now to think of sleep
It's best to just let go.

Will watch a class, let night-time come
And then go walk the dog.
Watch Venus and the Jupiter
Rise in the western sky.

Evening's a time to just slow down
Forget the stress of day.
Let go the weight that holds you down
And wait for sleep to come.

Glen Wasson
March 7, 2023

#694
Wednesday

A morning in the courtyard
Gliding back and forth.
Listening to the babbling brook
Only feet away.

Looking up the sky is blue
With few clouds now about.
Contrails streaking east and west
Rushing here and there.

No wind today, the sun is warm
A comfort I now feel.
Would wish that every day would be
As nice as is today.

The pidgins have a fountain too
Where they both drink and bathe.
Enjoying life as they've been given
A place where we observe.

This is the life retirement gives
No duties to the world.
Mind your business, tend your ways
A let live kind of life.

Each day is something new to me
A chance to think about.
To think about how life once was
And wait for more to come.

Glen Wasson
March 8, 2023

#696
Life As We Age

Are we to keep on living
And taking every breath?
No matter of the time we've spent
On this old spinning globe.

Are we allowed just so much time
To use all the resources?
Must we contribute to the cause,
Be worthy of the air?

Do older people have a place
Or should we give it up?
To someone stronger, abler too
Who'll contribute day by day.

Of course we once contributed
As all the young ones do.
We worked and paid our taxes too
And blessed the world with kids.

Now most of us are past our prime
Have passed into retirement.
No longer do the nine to five
More like the ten to three.

We like to eat and sleep and rest
That busy life we live.
Are mostly weak where we were strong
Is there a place for us?

When we were young and raising kids
And in the prime of life,
We never thought of getting old
No, never thought of that.

Allowed, are we still allowed to breathe
And use the limited
Resources that are left on earth,
How should we share them now?

Throughout my life did little harm
Was never very wasteful.
Always worked, contributed
Was always able to.

But now am in competing mode
I'm taking more than giving.
Will they still deem me worthy of
The things I need to live?

Not mine to do, in other hands
No longer my control.
Hope to be a worthy one
And live to see tomorrow.

Glen Wasson
March 10, 2023

#697
A Sad Poem

Why can't I write a sad, sad poem
Why am I always happy?
So many others write that way
I wonder why I can't?

I read the ones with sorrow and death
And drugs and rape and slaughter.
But I am stuck with "That's so nice."
I wonder why I can't?

I too have lived and have a life
But not at all like that.
Have not gone hungry, homeless too
My families always there.

I have experienced many things
Have moved and worked and loved.
But never like these others have
I see more joy than grief.

I also look at life in ways
That show it's better side.
I'm looking up, not looking down
I like to view the sky.

It's usually blue in Yuma town
Don't have too many clouds.
It's easy to enjoy yourself
To see the world like that.

I tend to be the happy sort
Though some will ask, "What's wrong?"
Depression runs within my veins
It sometimes pushes through.

My view of life is different from
Those other kinds of people.
I sit and contemplate the world
Let nature take it's course.

I sit in glider, back and forth
And listen to the brook.
I watch the birds fly to and fro,
They seem so free to me.

Perhaps ignore what I don't like
And let it pass me by.
"Don't want no irritants my way!"
I'd rather stay away.

Some people let the slightest thing
Offend their simple ways
And huff and puff and stew a while
And show their hot red face.

I only hurt the ones I love
Respect most all the others.
A trait I'm finding hard to break
It is my greatest fault.

Why can't I fix my greatest fault
And treat them all with love?
I say "I love you." yes I do
But hard to walk the walk.

The title now is far away,
I left it long ago.
But still I wonder why I can't
Express myself that way?

Glen Wasson
March 16, 2023

#699
I Remember

I remember when
When I was young and growing.
I sometimes wish that I'd advance
And get beyond this place.

I remember moving 'bout
That's how I passed my time.
I moved and found another state
A new school and new house.

Changing homes and changing schools
And changing businesses.
A lot of change in ten, twelve years
More than the friends I had.

I moved again, had family near
We'd visit back and forth.
But Sunday was a working day
They had to come to us.

I moved again, again, again
I now had reached high-school.
I got a job and wanted more
I wanted transportation.

I bought a motor scooter, yes
I rode it for a year.
Then I bought a Buick car
It was quite big and black.

This covers eight-teen years of life
This much I do remember.
So much of life I still will tell
Leave for another time.

Glen Wasson
March 19, 2023

#700
A Flood

How deep does the water need to be
To even be called a flood?
If it's in the street or in your house
If it's now waist deep to you?

Is it standing still or flowing brisk,
Is it moving things about?
Is the water clear or full of mud
Is it trying to take you down?

We all enjoy a little stream
One gently flowing by.
A home to fish and water-plants
The way that things should be.

How can this gentle stream become
A raging, flooding torrent?
Destroying banks and streets and homes
Bringing even death.

The water rises o'er the banks
And spreads across the plain.
Envelops all it meets in time
And sometimes moves it on.

Where are the dams and levees too
That were to control all this?
Are they working well or not at all?
Are they a total waste?

We all would say "Not in my home!
Don't want it near to me!"
Please let the water go to rest
Somewhere downstream from me.

It will recede, return to banks
The banks that once contained
The gentle little stream I liked,
That was so good to me.

The waters gone, the mud remains
It always leaves a mess.
For someone working hard to live
Within the flooded plain.

Scrape up the mess, haul it away
Repair the streets and fences.
Wash down with clear, clean water now
And make it like before.

In ample time it all will be
A distant memory.
Something to remember, but not desire
And never want again.

Glen Wasson
March 19, 2023

#701
Yuma

The sky is blue, it usually is
We live in Yuma town.
We love blue sky, perhaps some clouds
That's why we live down here.

It's March and spring has sprung in town
Shirtsleeves, no jacket needed.
The days are in the seventies plus
The nights are slightly cooler.

Within a month they will be gone
The snowbirds, winter visitors.
And leave our little, quiet town
To those who live year round.

By May the summer heat will come
The heat keeps most away.
One-hundred-ten to one-fifteen
We'll have five months of that.

But all that time blue sky will rule
And some occasional clouds.
We all enjoy the A.C. on
At home and in the car.

October comes, they will return
All those who hate the snow.
They come for six months of nice temps
And leave when it gets hot.

Glen Wasson
March 20,2023

#702
A Sonnet Without Rhymes

14 lines
Iambic Pentameter

The western sky is gray and dark to me
The trees are silhouetted black against
The sky that darkens as the sun recedes
The sun has little time to make its mark.
How can I see all that is left to see?
The darkness overtakes the bit that's left
The night is coming, daylight's nearly gone
So little time and light is left to see.
It's like a veil that covers over all
And all that seemed so real just hours ago
The silhouettes are all that's left to see
And soon they too will fade into the night.
The end is near, not much to look out for
No more to write, will have to end it here.

Glen Wasson
March 21, 2023

#703
Peace

The peaceful quiet of sound
The sound of a waterfall,
The sound of a gentle, babbling brook,
The silent sounds of day.

These peaceful sounds of day
Surround me in the courtyard.
All day round they come and go
Water's a gentle sound.

Why is peaceful nice?
What do we desire?
The end of day will bring more peace
Allow us to repose.

I rest in sun and listen
Enjoy this bit of time,
Times like these are few to see,
Perhaps will see tomorrow.

Glen Wasson
March 24, 2023

#704
The Chair

Have you ever sat in a chair that sets
In a particular place in space?
One who's view is the same each day
It never, ever, changes.

I have a chair I just described
It's in the near dog park.
I go there in the morn and eve
I have to walk the dog.

The view I see is clear to me
I see some trees and buildings.
And farther off some buildings rise
Above the ones about.

A hospital, that is what they are,
They have a copter too.
So red-lights sit upon there tops
To guide the copter in.

The lights, of course, are on at night
The buildings show as black.
But they are white in daylight time
That is the view I see.

But what I wrote is far away
The scene, it is quite small.
The buildings near are big and tall
And take up most the view.

The trees I see are really tall
And sorta have no shape.
Tall and gangling describes them well
For timber they are nil.

So that's my chair in which I sit
I sit and ponder much.
What's beyond the view I see,
Does it have an effect on me?

Glen Wasson
March 24, 2023

#705
Another Window

I take a look through a window that
Looks out on something different.
The window's in a different room
Away from normal view.

The pane of glass that covers it
Keeps out the wind and cold.
But freely lets me look outside
And see what is out there.

I see a courtyard from above
Not from the level ground.
Not sitting in a glider swing
I'm sitting in a chair.

It's interesting, a different view
To see things from above.
Not feel or hear the outside things
Can only take a look.

See people walking, know not where
They simply go their way.
Do this, do that, what ever they want
Another view of life.

Does it make much sense to wonder why
These others go about?
Their lives that have no meaning for me
I have no need to know.

Glen Wasson
March 27, 2023

#706
Blurb

My book: *New Poetry by an Old Man*

<u>Non-Poets:</u> If you are looking for little, short stories that fit upon a page, written in a narrative style that begins, continues and ends, try my poems in four line paragraphs. There's little if any rhyme to see, it's mostly life as I see it at 83 years.
<u>Poets:</u> Much tetrameter and trimeter alternating lines with occasional changes in form and meter. While the form looks like traditional Blank Verse, there are few rules found in my poems as I enjoy writing in flowing metrical style.

Glen Wasson

#707
Blue Skies

This must be 'bout tenth time said
"There's blue skies over Yuma!"
But truth be told, that's how it is
Most always a blue sky.

'Tis end of March, a few days left
We've had the winds and rain.
Within a month they'll all be gone
Our annual winter guests.

By then the summer heat will come
It will be hot and hotter.
And only we who live year round
Will smile a gentle smile.

Our population will settle down
About one hundred thou.
Some restaurants and businesses
Will close down for a while.

But blue skies, like I said before,
Will rule the sky each day.
To grow the crops we're noted for
And ship them far away.

Glen Wasson
March 28, 2023

#708
Contrails

There are no clouds up in the sky
Just contrails made by jets.
They usually fly from west to east
This seems to be their path.

These people going back and forth
From one coast to the other,
The population going forth
To keep the nation level.

They seem to be so very small
Way up there far beyond.
Now only can we wonder why
They all are flying where?

While on the ground they look so large
These planes that fly so high.
But when they are in their domain
They always look so tiny.

Sometimes I wonder why I think
About such simple thoughts,
But someone has to wonder why
Cause others to believe.

A worry-wort, someone would say
I worry about nothing.
It's just a poets mind at work
To think where others don't.

I always had an interest in
The world of planes and such.
At eighteen took a lesson to
Learn to fly a Cub.

That was a cold and windy day
Sometime in winter time.
I only logged a half an hour
And never took another.

But I remember like it was
Not so many years
I took my money, paper route,
And took that fateful flight.

These are thoughts that follow you
Continue through your life.
They're nice to come across like this
And let you reminisce.

Here's to life and all of it
The good, the bad, the ugly.
Tuck those memories deep back there
And visit now and then.

Glen Wasson
March 31, 2023

#709
Night

Night is black as we look out
The sun is now long gone.
The silhouettes that sunset gave
Are no longer in sight.

With city lights, no stars in sight
The simple ghost of gray.
The sounds close down as darkness comes
The sounds of day are gone.

The lights in windows, one by one
Have ceased to shine tonight.
Before the sun begins to rise
They will be turning on.

The quiet of the night will fade
As daylight starts to glow.
And daylight life begins to move
With people and their work.

Day and night, light and dark
As opposite they are,
Controls the days and nights we have
Continue on and on.

Glen Wasson
March 31, 2023

#710
Alliteration or Greek Tantogram?

Just some thoughts I had about using words in an interesting way.

Wistfully wandering, while walking with Walters walker, Willy wondered whether Wanda would wait woefully while we wilted?

Glen Wasson
April 3, 2023

#711
Life Repeating

Why does life repeat itself?
Why do we suffer more?
So life, the better it will be
To open window wide.

Open wide, let the light shine in
Expose us to all nature.
Life is not just us alone
But every one out there.

Have taken two trips so far today
One for breakfast, one for dog
And each exposed me to the air
The sun, the sky, the all.

After more than eighty years
I've met life here and there.
Sometimes by choice, sometimes by chance
Sometimes by simply being.

Those who are young do not know yet
All that the world holds forth.
Will come to face what all will be
Life is all that we have.

Glen Wasson
April 1, 2023

#712
Same

So much the same, no difference now
The days are much the same.
Blue sky, no clouds, it's all the same
Is this a boring life?

As one retired I see no change
Each day is like the last.
So what do I desire of life,
Do I desire a change?

Perhaps I'm set in all my ways
Will not accept a change?
Beneath it all, a stubborn one
I walk a study path.

As much as I believe in change
My life is pretty dull.
Get up, go eat, recline to rest,
And do it once again.

As one retired, I've found my place
Not many things to do.
I guess I live a simple life
Not much I have to do.

I will repeat this once again
All when the morn appears.
Will try to find purpose in life
Put on a friendly smile.

Glen Wasson
April 1, 2023

#713
A Poets Life

Thoughts and wonders, wandering mind
Plotting, dwelling, searching near
Life is such to a poets self
Seeing life as it comes to him.

He could sit and wait for it,
Come embrace him, touch his heart
Send his way a scent at dawn
Call his ear at evening time.

Taste the world with all it has
Take it's wonder as it comes
This is life as it comes to man
Not to others—hold their hand.

Be a gift or curse to him
Blessing, take and hold and feel
Let them nourish, feed and grow
Wish to harvest, need to sow.

Writing when the words that come
Fall as ink, the pen is full
Line by line they fill the page
Find some meaning, what is there.

If outside, the air is felt
Brisk or subtle, cold or warm
Trees and birds, clouds and sky
Nature in its full display.

Write those words and fill those lines
Rhymes and metaphors will bloom
Bring some imagery to light
Bring it forth with all your might.

Glen Wasson
April 7, 2023

#716
The Sky Today

The sky today is sorta gray
Would say it's overcast.
Not really clouds up in the sky
More like a washed up gray.

For Yuma, this is not the way,
It should be blue each day.
With few, if any, clouds to see
Just blue, a deep, deep blue.

Don't look for rainy days out here,
Get water from the river.
And grow crops two, three times a year.
Few places are like here.

As summer comes it does get hot,
One hundred-ten and more.
Only us hard ones stay about
The others head back north.

But if you want your vegetables
And want your cotton too,
You'd best remember Yuma town
Cause that's where it comes from.

Glen Wasson
April 12, 2023

#717
Lotsa

Lotsa, lotsa, lotsa.
Lotsa time to spend.
Lotsa life to live.
Lotsa friends to have.

Lotsa time to spend,
A little spent each day.
Time will slip away,
Can never get it back.

Lotsa life to live,
Our life just once to live.
Don't want to lose our life,
Will live it cautiously.

Lotsa friends to have
Have many when you're young.
You want some, hold them close,
Will be there when in need.

Lotsa time and life and friends
To use, abuse or lose.
Too late in time have wasted them
And then will be alone.

Glen Wasson
April 21, 2023

#718
What Would You Be

What would you be if you weren't,
Weren't the way you were today?
Would you want to change the way you were
Or would you stay the same?

Wouldn't you rather revise yourself,
To be different than what you were?
To be able to see yourself that way,
The way you'd want to be?

Change is how we move ourselves
From what we are to what we want.
To show the world we're not in a rut
To show them we can change.

But what if we really are in a rut
With only one way to go?
What if we couldn't move left or right,
Had no control of direction?

Is this all that our lives have become,
Just yesterday, today, tomorrow?
With no variation, direction or change
Life has to be more than this.

When life begins we are growing,
Developing in all new ways.
Becoming what we someday will be
To grow and live our lives.

Growing, living, becoming more,
Becoming what we will be.
When we mature to age twenty-one
We cease to grow in stature.

We may grow fat or lose a few,
We may learn skills or study.
We may grow a family or loose some old ones
Our lives will never just be.

Our lives are for living, what ever that is
Living our lives as they come.
Some will be good, some will be bad
That'll be the lives we live.

Glen Wasson
April 23, 2023

#719
Spring Is Gone

The end of April, drawing near
The air is silent and soft.
There is no sound to reach my ear
No bit of life to loft.

Cool mornings soon will cease to be
The days will soon be hot.
The sun is all that we shall see
The coolness will be hot.

In Yuma that's the way it is
Will soon be hot and hotter.
In Ag is where the business is
And that will be the bother.

Till the soil and wet the seed
And tend the weeds and such.
The second crop will soon take heed
The vegies will be much.

In Yuma that is how it is
We live on fertile soil.
Commercial land is for the biz
If on the beach, be sand.

Glen Wasson
April 27, 2023

#720
Yuma

We wait and wait for spring to come
And now it turns to summer.
Was nice and cool for oh, so long
And now it's simply hot.

We have no snow and little rain
That's just the way it is.
They must have come in winter time
To think they'd live year round.

They came from somewhere way up north
To think this was the place.
Were tired of scooping snow and ice,
Decided to try this.

It turned out to be great for them
It treated them so well.
The river was a snow melt stream
Supplying all their needs.

Who knew what all the crops would be
Some vegetables and wheat
And cotton, alfalfa too
To number just a few.

It took a wise and thinking man
To think that it would work.
To till the soil and plant the seed
With water that was snow.

To see the land untilled and bare
It took a lot of courage.
To give up fertile land up north
And move into a desert.

To visualize a water scheme
To irrigate the crops.
To share the water far away
They now wish that they hadn't.

Over the years some dams were built
To stop the yearly floods.
And tame the flow of a precious gift
Provide a place to play.

So many people claim that gift
The gift of precious water.
To water crops and drink it down
And even water lawns.

Perhaps quite soon will have to save
Conserve the melted gift.
And spread it wide for all to use
And peaceful neighbors be.

Glen Wasson
April 27, 2023

#722
It's Night

It's night out here in courtyard
It's quiet, still and strange.
It's strange cause all is seeking out
What is this night about?

The sky is dark but stars don't shine
The city lights too much.
Is still quite warm at eighty-five
Will only cool a bit.

It's summer time in Yuma town
Will now be hot and hotter.
The snowbirds all have flown away
Back to their northern climes.

The sky's all blue, clouds few or none
Like almost every day.
The visitors are few when hot
They only stop for gas.

A.C. has made it livable
They used to use a cooler.
But some must work outside all day
They are the toughest ones.

Our Yuma town will never be
A sunny beach to lay
But some seek out the river cool
A refuge from the heat.

Glen Wasson
April 28, 2023

#723
Walkers, Scooters and Canes

Walkers, scooters and canes
Are aids to getting about.
They keep you study when standing up
And safe from falling down.

Not everybody uses one
Not everyone has needs.
But for those who have a need
They are a welcome sight.

When getting old a cane may be
The first aid that you need.
It gives three points to study you
To reassure your stance.

A walker with two wheels in front
Allows both hands to hold.
The ones with four wheels better yet
They let the user sit.

The scooters top the list of all
The aid a person needs.
With 'lectric power, speed is king
They zoom about the place.

Glen Wasson
April 29, 2023

#724
Breezy

It's breezy today in Yuma town
The sky has scattered clouds.
I hear the wind as it fondles the trees,
The wind caresses the leaves.

The first of May and summer has come
No longer mornings are cool.
We feel it as we open the door
No more the cool will be.

Our visitors are mostly gone
They now will go back north.
To summers they are accustomed to
Not like what we have here.

We are the hardened ones down here
The ones who live year round.
Who like the small town feel we have
When all of them are gone.

They come with ninety thou or more
Double our population.
Our streets are not designed for them
Sometimes a mighty jam.

But again each year we welcome them
They bring their trucks and trailers.
And fill up all the R.V. Parks
And live for five months here.

It's never quite the same with them
And all their license plates
They wear their shorts and tee shirt tops
And feel that it is warm.

For most of us who live year round
It's time for coats and jackets.
We think of summer when its hot
And yes, we think it's cold.

From now on it will just be hot
Well hot and often hotter.
With our A.C. Its comfortable
We take it's part of life.

Until October this will be
A quiet desert town.
Few visitors will come this way
And fewer still will stay.

Glen Wasson
May 1, 2023

#725
Prison Hill

The first time I came to Prison Hill
Was May of Nineteen-Seventy-Six.
Was driving home from old L.A.
In Yuma it was hot.

We had two boys of six and eight
Had been to Bible School.
Would spend the summer in Norman, O.K.
And then go down to Dallas.

Prison Hill was hot and dry
The cells looked more like caves.
Would not be nice to spend time there
Would surely seem like Hell.

The museum was cool and interesting
It showed what life was like.
I'm sure the guards felt badly too
To live in Yuma heat.

When we completed our little tour
Returned to our locked car.
The avocado we had raised
Was now a wilted tree.

We could not wait to leave this town
More like a winter guest.
I never thought that back in time
That I'd be living here.

Glen Wasson
May 1, 2023

#726
A Bit of Yuma in Summer

In summertime our town will change
From what it is in winter.
First off there's fewer people here
More like a desert town.

In winter population grows
To almost double size.
But most of them can't take the heat
And quickly move back north.

They ask us how we take the heat,
We tell them "That's the way!"
We know it's hot so take things slow
And spend most time inside.

Our homes are air-conditioned now
Our cars and work the same.
We know to spend our lives inside
Not out there in the sun.

From San Diego we're half way
To that large Phoenix town.
Three hours either way you go
It's Interstate both ways.

To visit others it's a trip
Few people live close by.
This southwest corner few can take
But grows most winter crops.

If winter lived here all year round
Would have a million people.
All living the great winter clime
Would mostly all be old.

We mostly like our desert town
That's why we live year round.
It takes a certain person type
To say that you enjoy it.

Michelle and I we have two rooms
That open on a courtyard.
With trees, fake grass and fountain too
We have all we need.

We have a dog, Bucky's his name
We walk him morn and night.
We stay inside our A.C.ed rooms
And take our meals in stride.

What can I say, we like it here
Here in our Yuma town.
I've lived here over twenty years
And soon will be a native.

Glen Wasson
May 1, 2023

#727
I Sat in the Warmth

I sat in the sun all surrounded by warmth
I sat there without any care.
No care in the world did I have in my mind
Was totally without a fear.

As spring draws to close and the summer awaits
The warmth will become only hot.
The A.C. turns on just to cool our abode
The door will be most often closed.

The temps soon will reach our one hundred and more
And stay that way most of the day.
To grow all the crops that surround our small town
And drink of the rivers cool gift.

The snowbirds enjoy all the winter and spring
Not facing the snow and the ice.
Relaxing in sun that's not seen way up north
But waiting to go way back home.

But some of us live here, yes all the year round
Do not retreat up north like them.
Enjoy now our little bare desert region
When there's just us locals around.

We now find a place that just fits our own style
Somewhere that we sit and relax.
Will suffer through all of the summers dry heat
Await all the winters cool air.

Glen Wasson
May 8, 2023

#728
Small Booklets

I'm writing small booklets, the pages are few
They number just four eight or twelve.
Contain mostly poems I have written before
But sometimes a new one appears.

Have one to send to all the teachers and schools
And one for our own Y.S.L.
Another is called by Philosophy name
For those who do just sit and wonder.

I wrote one just for the old Prison Hill place
The visitors center right there.
There's poems about our little bare desert town
And other rare facts they should know.

I've written one for all the folks who now grieve
Who suffer from sickness and death.
To let them know that they are never alone
And try to convey hope and cheer.

I've bought a new stapler with saddle to hold
All the sheets that I've folded in half.
And cutter to trim all the other three sides
A scale to weigh all that I send.

I know that I won't get rich off of my sales
It may be a hobby for now.
But I will enjoy all the effort I've spent
To share all my poems just with you.

Glen Wasson
May 8, 2023

#753
Happy

*Seven beats to the line, Heptameter with a
Trochee first line and Iamb second line.*

Happy, happy, happy is the man who pays his bills
With the effort he puts forth or with the sum he has.

Happy, happy, happy is the wife who rules the house
Who births the babes and nurses them and gives them loving care.

Happy, happy, happy is the farmer of the land
Who tills the soil with faith to grow and tends the stock with care.

Happy, happy, happy is the merchant in the town
Who buys the stock he hopes to sell and tends the customer.

Happy, happy, happy are the children of the town
Who frolic gaily every day and get to school on time.

Happy, happy, happy is the village and the farms
That gather on a Sunday morn to sing and pray to God.

Joyful are the people who make up this area
They do depend on everyone who gather as a one.

Glen Wasson
May 22, 2023

#754
Blue Sky

Blue sky, blue sky, blue sky
Always blue skies over Yuma.
Hardly ever a cloud is seen
Always blue skies over Yuma.

But that is why we are here
We stay here all year round.
Always blue skies over Yuma
That's why they fly from here.

The Marines fly planes both day and night
Three-hundred-sixty-five.
Almost always good to fly
Almost always good.

A lot of repetition here
A lot of on and on.
We always know what tomorrow will bring
The same as yesterday.

Things don't change in Yuma town
They always stay the same.
Can never have too much of good
There's only one down-side.

In summer time it does get hot
And then gets even hotter.
That grows the crops that make it green
Good thing we have the river.

In truth we are a bit diverse
We come from many sides.
We have the crops, the air base too
And thousands spend the winter.

In summer you look round and see
The old and hardened ones.
Who live here the whole year around,
The ones who call it home.

For those who travel through and leave
A green spot on the map.
With sand-dunes here and desert there
They often wonder why.

Why would you live two hundred miles
From any city place?
There's Phoenix, San Diego too
We're just a gas stop here.

We have our times, there's one or two
Hot air balloons and cars.
A hundred thousand come and go
And don't forget the dunes.

A quarter million I've been told
Thanksgiving weekend long.
Their campfires burn for miles around
A playground made of sand.

There's things to see out in the sand
A plank-road and some graves.
They speed around and jump the dunes
And drink a lot of beer.

But here in town there's Shell and me
And Bucky dog makes three.
We live in what we call our home
Enjoy our later years.

And all about blue skies above
Above the fertile soil.
We all need somewhere to call home
And Yuma is our home.

Glen Wasson
May 26, 2023

#755
How Do YOU Spell Yukaliptuss?

I pose it as a question
It certainly is to me.
A tree that grows in the southwest of
The good old U.S.A.

I first encountered them when young
About the age of seven.
We moved from state where I was born
To golden California.

I still equate that tree with sea
That salty scent sea air.
It smells like nothing I have smelt
A pleasant memory.

But back to tree of question
It's tall and gangally..
It's never straight but always bent
And twisted every way.

For a young Nebraska boy it was
Unusual to behold.
But everything when you're that age
Is something of a wonder.

I spelt the name, I sounded it
I also had some fun.
I do enjoy life at my age
Enjoy a laugh or two.

I have a dictionary,
I also have a phone,
I know that I could say into
That word that I can't spell.

I also have a microwave
Computer, printer too.
All things that came to me as new
I've been around that long.

But what does this all have to do
With that tall and gangally tree?
That I can't spell without some help
Eucalyptus.

Glen Wasson
May 27, 2023

#756
Changing a Tire

I grew up when the roads were rough
And nails were often present.
The tires were not so good back then
They always had a tube.

A simple nail became a flat
And happened quite a bit.
You pulled unto the side of road
And opened up the trunk.

Got out the jack and spare tire too
This was the 1940s.
If it was hot the family got
To stand beside the road.

There was a rod we called "Tire iron"
That had a double job.
It popped the hubcap off the wheel
And pumped the jack up high.

That same tire iron was used to turn
The nuts that held the wheel.
The nuts were put in that hubcap
So's not to be lost in weeds.

With spare in hand we changed the tire
(You never changed "The wheel")
Reverse all that you did before
You knew the process well.

You closed the trunk
And entered the car
And looked for a place to fix the flat.

But every little station
With a gas pump right outside
Could, and would, perform the task
And charge a small, small fee.

They had "Cold" patches and also "Hot"
The hot held on better
Unto the tube within the tire,
Was quite an operation.

Those were the days when a trip became
A real adventure too.
You drove at forty, forty-five
The windows open wide.

And every trip included one or two
Flat tires, they weren't so good.
Just be glad was not blown out
Would have to buy another.

Glen Wasson
May 27, 2023

#757
5 o'clock

It's five o'clock, sun in the west
The shadows long and dark.
Though still quite warm, the sky is blue
In Yuma, always blue.

I sit and glide both back and forth
It's just a little bit.
I greet the few that pass me by
In general, just enjoy.

It's hard to write about the change
When change does not occur.
We live in Yuma, all the same
Could simply be a postcard.

I know that change is happening
It really has to be.
But all of it just seems the same
As life goes slowly by.

Glen Wasson
May 27, 2023

#758
Our Lives

Anapest Tetrameter/Trimeter
Two unstressed syllables followed by a stressed syllable
Four feet (beats) per line / three feet per line

I finish my meal and I slip out the door
And walk past the babaling brook.
Continue to walk to the glider I seek
And carefully set myself down.

I close both my eyes and enjoy the new view
The view that now rest's in my mind.
Results of the life I have already lived
That's what we old people can do.

Our memories are but a part of our lives
A part that we never forget.
A part that we mostly just want to keep real
But some we'd just like to forget.

Enjoying our life as it now comes to us
It is the best part we can do.
Our main part of life has now passed us right by
We now have the short end of life.

To be that young one and just starting out life
And have it all out there to live.
That we now can leave to the young ones to live
We all did the best that we could.

Our lives are a bit of the time we have lived
So much time has already passed.
So much will remain after we all are gone
For somebody else to live through.

Glen Wasson
May 29, 2023

#759
More Of Blue

I'm thinking of the color blue
The color of the sky.
I see it every day of life
It's always up above.

I live in what is called Yuma
We live right on the river.
The river's not as blue as sky
But waters all the crops.

For you who've lived in Yuma town
You know what blue skies are.
They are the ones you see all day
All day, most every day.

They are so blue, so blue they are
They carry not a cloud.
Bring joy to us who look skyward
Will never disappoint.

That's just the way it is in town
Surrounded by the crops.
From up above the desert's green
The river keeps it green.

To see the produce that comes forth
You know why farmers came.
The fertile soil and sun so bright
A farmers sure delight.

But many are retired and old
No longer produce work.
We put in efforts years ago
And now rest on our past.

We know it's hot in summer time
And drives out many folks.
Who come from cooler pastures north
They just enjoy our winter.

Look up, observe the sky so blue
How could you ever leave.
This place that blesses you each day
With wonders to behold.

We thank you Yuma, people too
Who welcome many more.
To show us what nice weather is
And shares it with the world.

Glen Wasson
May 30, 2023

My Booklet
My Life and the Weather in Yuma

My Book
New Poetry by an Old Man

#760
Ocean To Ocean Bridge

We have upon our shores right here
The Ocean To Ocean Bridge.
It connects both East and West
To make the Continent whole.

For fifteen years roads had been built
Allowing cars to travel.
But halted in the West by one
The Rocky Mountain range.

The roads were more like trails back then
To cross they used a ferry.
It must have been a dusty trip
With open cars the mode.

And to the West there were the dunes
The sweltering, dusty, dunes.
Not quite the playground of today
They were a daunting task.

To build a road of planks,
All held together at the time
with iron straps and some spikes.

The wind would blow, the sand would shift
The road would start to move.
From time to time a man and team
Would pull it back in place.

Glen Wasson
June 1, 2023

#762
Sneezing

All in the air is the pollen so sweet
Falling from trees where the birds sit and tweet.
Liking a sneeze that is surely to come
Waiting—waiting--it surely will come.

Bring forth your handkerchief, cover your mouth
Dab at your nose, it dribbles a bit.
Hay fever has got you, you'll never be free
Sneezing and dabbing and blowing your nose.

Is it only in spring when the flowers appear
Or does it continue through seasons to come?
A drip and a dab, then repeat it again
Look out or it follows the rest of your life.

Glen Wasson
June 9, 2023

#763
My Back and Neck

My back and neck are bended down
My steps are short and quick.
Do not stride out as once I did
Have met my elder life.

When climbing stairs I use the rail
At least with one lone hand.
The left hand matches my right leg
I think that's like a cane.

You look at me as I did them
I wondered bought my elders.
What they did them what's I do now
Must be what life's about.

I guess I'm normal for my age
I'm living out my life.
In ways I never thought I would
Would be an old, old man.

Glen Wasson
June 15, 2023

#764
Oh, To Be Like Them

Why are they so famous, those who came before
Who came and wrote from times gone by
Who knew of life we don't?

Where did they learn of life so real
While we just seem to live by days?
Are we to know what they just knew
Or do we have to live and learn?

Do we need to suffer much as they did in their lives,
Or can we learn from how they lived and build on what they said?
Is life too simple as we now live, too simple to just learn,
Too simple to demand of us what was required of them?

We have so much to live too well, above all that we need.
Are we too weak to stand up straight and face the world we meet?
Or can we truly say we've lived when nothing caused us grief?
Breath deep, breath long, take it all in, fulfill what we don't know.

Has life been too good to us, to suffer all they did?
Must we face the bad they saw in life, to truly see the good?
Do we miss nature as they lived, they lived and looked and
wondered?
Our life is soft, we have no strength, we have no will to live.

They struggled, lived, wrote and thought, why can't we do the
same?
Their struggle made them who they were, the greatest of them all.
They wrote of life as we don't see, life was harder then.
No wonder we don't write as they, their lives were different then.

Did they have ways of living then, that we don't have today?
Did they earn the fame they got in ways that we cannot?
Was life more conducive to writing then than what it is today?
Do we have a chance to write as they have written way back then?

Are tears of sorrow and tears of shame required to make us real?
Must we stub toes on rocks and cracks and bleed upon the ground?
Contribute that that only we can offer at this time?
Is more required than what I said, more then I'm set to give?

Today I am but an old man, I've only thoughts, questions and
memories.
Answers are so few to come, they seem to hide and cloak
themselves.
And not present themselves as words or sounds, but shadows dark
and gray.
Why don't words just come to me the way they came to them?

Must I present my naked breast to all the swords, slings and
arrows?
That all my enemies posses and are prepared to use at will?
Is that what it takes to be a man of letters, thoughts and poems?
Will I survive what life has for me, as one who's not prepared?

May I who sits in cooled room when it's oh, so hot outside?
I suffer not as they did then, I suffer not as some do now!
I live a very privileged life, I do, a life that's all so good.
I suffer not in ways of want, I have no needs to dwell upon.

I may not suffer what I must, to reach for fame so far,
My simple resources are not like theirs, I hardly ever walk!
The streams of water flowing by were only built by men.
My nature now is not like theirs, all wild and rough and real.

They looked at not we as it came, with little man had changed
But made some walls and cleared some roads and humble houses
built.
There were the hills, the valleys too, trees and rivers flowed on by.
The rain clouds gathered overhead but they could only guess what
it would bring.

With quills they wrote with ink they made on paper bought in
town.
It was required of those who sought a higher class to reach
To read and write and figure too and learn to speak with voice.
Today we all so little learn, are we even allowed to say we are
learned?

Yes I want to reach that peak of elevated voices
Like those who speak above all that and that above the din.
Is it just noise that I have made with all my feeble efforts?
Do I then speak for those who read my words in lines and stanzas,
Or do I yet speak for those who will in some unknown time?

My eyes, they strain against the page, I also wear my glasses.
My mind, it wanders like my steps, and not in a straight line.
My ears hear ringing that's not there but move it out of sight.
The strength I have is not like that I had when I was young.

Will I fail to reach my goal, to write like they once did
Or am I now a has been guy who started out too late?
Will my dull words that reach your ears instill a thought or two,
Cause you to pause a bit or two to dwell on what I mean?

Glen Wasson
June 17, 2023

Written after watching an hour course on *Poets of The Romantic Period.*

#765
Fitness

I must admit I'm not as fit
As I was when I was younger.
I used to walk and run and play
As I was back in that day.

Even today don't look my age
They think I'm somewhat younger.
They are mistaken, I really am
The old man standing here.

I was born in what was the thirties
And now we're in the twenties.
I'm closer to the century mark
Than I was some years ago.

But I've done a lot in my now long life
I've seen and smelled and heard.
We have five senses, use them well
They tell us what we know.

I have seen things that those today
Can only sit and wonder.
I've seen a lot of change since I
First came upon this earth.

My folks were born two centuries ago
Twas in the eighteen hundreds.
They'd be about one thirty now
If they had lived this long.

Dad fought in the war to end all wars
Now called the First World War
And then we had a fiercer one
That killed some millions more.

And World War Two didn't end things then
Have been fighting most ever since.
Mankind can only be that way
Don't seem to like our neighbors.

But we still rise and exercise
We try to look so fit
We sweat and strain and bend and stretch
And even lift some weights.

Why can't we just look fit and clean
Why must we fight these wars?
Would be much cheaper to just grow food
Than building guns and bombs.

We often blame our folks we do
"My dad does this!" "Your dad does that!"
As if it makes a difference
But we must stand for what we said
And pick up stones to throw.

"I'll do push-ups to build my arms
So I can throw bigger stones.
And later on build bigger guns
To blast your peaceful home.

Maybe we should all be weak
Too weak to shoot and throw.
And only use bad words to say
"I hate you so and so!"

Glen Wasson
June 19, 2023

#766
Clouds

The wispy clouds float in the blue
The blue sky canopy.
When looking up it's all you see
This blue sky canopy.

What changes day by day up there
But wispy clouds and more?
Most always just the same each day
We have a stable clime.

It's sunny every day it is
Few clouds, if any, there.
The growing season's very long
So many days each year.

The temps they climb in summer time
Most every day it's hot.
And then it gets more hotter still
Rids us of all the weak.

The river near provides the soil
With what it needs to grow
The crops for which we're known for,
The leafy vegetables.

But those grow mostly in winter time
The coolest time we have.
The population grows then too
A hundred thousand more.

There's alfalfa, cotton, corn and wheat
They like the summer heat.
Those who live here all year round
Have learned to like it too.

Granted we live inside those months
When it's hundred ten and more.
But there are those who work outside
We have to say, "Thank You."

All you who live in cooler climes
May wonder why we're here.
We sorta like the place we live
The winter's all so nice.

A poet such as me,
Or is it "Such as I?"
Sit in a chair or at a desk
In A.C.'d luxury.

We never shovel snow down here
We never even see
That stuff that sends you all down here
The stuff that makes you flee.

That's why we all live way down here
So far from snow and ice.
We leave that to you hardy folk
That think that that is nice.

Glen Wasson
June 19, 2023

#767
Looking Down

As we age out we tend to look
More down than looking up.
We see the little steps we take
But seldom see the sky.

That is why it means so much
To sit and look around.
To see the things that surround us
And even see the sky.

Up there we see the clouds that float
Above the trees that sway
Above the birds that fly so high
So free, so free up there.

I like to sit in glider swing
Sit back, look up, around.
And let my troubles float away,
Don't really have that many.

Some say that life is what we make
It, make it good or bad.
But I desire to see the good
And let the bad slide by.

I too am old and looking down
I see my feet step out.
But fail to see what's right ahead
I seem to miss so much.

Our view of life is up to us
Look down and see ourselves.
Or raise our eyes and see the world
That rests there just out front.

See the birds and hear them chirp
Smell the flowers that grace our place.
Observe the people all about
And feel the sun on cheek.

There's lots of life to live and learn
We never know enough.
The world is changing fore our eyes
We only have to look.

We have our senses, five we have
To touch and hear and taste and smell and even see it all.
If you have five then thank the Lord
There's those who don't have all.

Make your life a joyful place
Look up and see it all.
Before you know will all be gone
Our life will have to end.

Glen Wasson
June 20, 2023

#768
Life as We Live It

Life, life as we live it
What is life but life lived.
Life, breathed and tasted in the day
Life lived as best we can.

Who can live this life that must be lived
To be experienced as only life can be?
Life is the itch that causes us to scratch
To scratch until we bleed our blood.

To scratch at life as only we can do is all
That life can give us, all that we can bear.
To live life without the itch that needs
Scratching, needs scratching to maintain the itch.

What is life without the itch that needs scratching
Scratching to get through the skin that protects
The flesh, the flesh that clings to the bone.
We are more than what we see.

What we see is the stone before the craftsman
Takes his chisel and chips away all the unneeded
Leaving an image that only he can see in his mind.
Life is what is left when the unneeded is gone.

How do we get to truly experience life?
Where does the itch come from?
Is life an itch or a scratch?
Do we know life when we experience it?

Life is more than breathing and feeling.
Life must demand more of us than simply living.
Life must be felt with all the senses, with all our might.
Life must be to be.

We may grow old without living life.
Are we simply staggering through life without
Meaning? Meaning must satisfy that itch that
Must be scratched, that must be endured.

What is life if we don't experience it to its fullest,
Felt, smelled, heard, tasted and seen?
We see life daily, touch it, hear the sounds.
What is life if we don't take it in its fullest?

Life is finite, it has a beginning, it has an end.
Is life worth living without a legacy?
What is legacy without pain and hurt?
Is life all joy without pain and hurt?

Life must be the pea under the mattresses!
Life must be the burr under the saddle!
Life must be the stone in the shoe!
Life must be the blister on the heel!

Life is more than just living, just being.
Life is joy and pain, knowing the one because of the other.
Life is being pulled and quartered.
Life is living in all that it has for us.

Many of us live life without experiencing it,
All life, no itch.
Life is itches and scratching and seeking relief,
Seeking relief from what life throws at us.

Only then can you say you have lived.
Only then is the itch scratched away in a pain.
Inflicted by our own hands to satisfy life.
Only by satisfying life have we lived it.

Do you feel lived? Have you scratched the itch?
Have you delved below the skin to feel the flesh below?
Have you felt the cold chisel and the hammer that strikes it?
Are you what life intended or just a work in progress?

Does life require too much, too much to be endured?
Does living life that way give us happiness or grief?
Does the ranting of this poet bring you hope?
Does life really need to be lived to be experienced?

Take my hand and let us go forth to see life!
Let us step beyond what we now have done
And let us, hand in hand, face the new life demanded of us.
A new life we will address with all the power within us.

Do you feel that itch, that before unknown feeling?
Shall we trod on or pause to scratch that itch?
A pause to give a moment of peace and comfort?
A moment in the life we are now experiencing?

Here we meet a crossroad, a choice we now must make?
We could stop here and not go on, but what would we
Have missed? Life is full of these testing times,
Go left, go right, stop and pause.

But life goes on even if we don't,
A life that was not lived.
Dare you say at your time of death
"I chose to pause and wait."

Life can be painful, yet exciting, exciting and joyful.
Joyfulness is living life for all it's worth!
Making it all worthwhile.
What do you choose?

Glen Wasson
June 20, 2023

#769
Words

What are words but letters and syllables
Strong and weak, beat and pause
Some are short and some are long
All have meaning or something to do

Within a poem a line of words will have a start and ending
Another line may follow close for lack of punctuation
An Em dash may be placed right here or in the middle of a line
To make the reader pause a bit before proceeding on.

Words may mean a lot of things, explain the reason why
Or ask a question, make a statement, call in that punctuation
The meaning of some words are clear while others are obscure
A dictionary's a handy tool, a thesaurus may be too

Words make up the news we read, with numbers the weather report
The songs we sing contain them too, as well as poems and books
These words are used by you and me to simply talk a bit
We simply can't communicate without the use of words

Words of anger and of love, triumphant and defeat
All use the same twenty-six of them, the letters we all use
With punctuation symbols too they tell us how to talk
Emphatic stops! And questions too? Mean something really
different

With words we can express ourselves, with anger, joy or grief
Emotions that we all can feel, be spoken or wrote down
Or simply facts we face each day with words we freely share
Too many to count, they fill all books and lectronic airways

Glen Wasson
June 24, 2023

#770
Cups and Glasses

A cup of coffee, cup of tea
A glass of milk or juice
Are ways to start the morning off
Beginning of your day.

You lift the cup and smell the brew
And take a sip of what it is.
A smile now goes across your lips
A smile to greet your day.

Your breakfast is your break fast time
It ends your night of rest.
It fuels you up for work to do
And start you on your way.

So here we are, go 'bout your day
Without a care or worry.
Another day of life to live
And joy within your heart.

Glen Wasson
June 25, 2023

#771
Again I Say it's Blue as Blue

I've said it more than once I have
"The sky is blue as blue."
This is the Yuma where I live
The sky is mostly blue.

Few clouds inhabit skies round here
You might say "Few and far."
That's why they fly their planes out here
The sky's most always blue.

I've lived here twenty-three years now
I guess I must enjoy it.
I know it's not for everyone
But once you're hooked, you're hooked.

The Summer Solstice just passed by
The temps have reached one hundred.
Will be the norm for quite some time
That's what it's like out here.

If not for water few would be
Within our little city
But rivers flow just North of us
And waters all our crops.

With this blue sky it seldom rains
Three inches a year is all
Then clouds clear out, it's blue again
The Sun, it rules 'ore all.

Glen Wasson
June 27, 2023

#772
Sundown

The sky that's mostly blue as blue
Has paled as evening nears.
The blue is pale and tending gold
The Sun a spot so bright.

The golden hew about the Sun
So gold, so bright, so glowing.
For a little while will be the sky
That was so blue so long.

For days we have three parts to see
There's morn and day and evening.
The morn announced the light to night
The day so blue will last so long
The evening oh, so brief.

But that is how it is right here
In our own little Yuma town.
Day after day it all comes round
A glorious day to love.

The Sun's now down, blue turns to black
And soon will all be gone.
To be repeated in the morn
Another Yuma day..

Glen Wasson
June 30, 2023

#773
Oh, To Think More Highly

Oh, to think more highly of oneself
Than one should really think.
Be humble, simple in desire
Know your true oneself.

Let the accolades come onto you
And do not reach for them.
If they are yours, will come to you
As something you deserve.

Our motives must be pure they must
Cannot give praise to self.
Must wait for it to find your place
To see just where you sit.

Oh, to grab the bright spotlight
Illuminate yourself.
But it must come from someone else
Never from yourself.

A proud one has so far to fall
The pedestal so high, so narrow.
Support must come outside yourself
And must be given you.

Harken to the cautious word
Do not lean out too far.
To topple is a simple thing
Recovery is in vain.

We like to elevate ourselves
Above the most of men.
Although we may have feet of clay
They're bound to let us down.

Do not stand tall and proud and feel
"The best is meant for me!"
Be humble, simple in your stance
Be quiet till the call.

If they want you the call will come
You need not seek it out.
To rule is not a goal to seek
But one to be declared.

Glen Wasson
July 2, 2023

#774
A Hint of Haze

A hint of haze that blew the blue
But still no hint of cloud.
The blues not like it was before
That hint of haze pervades.

Our Yuma skies are most the same
A bluer than blue, blue sky.
A cloud will hardly make the scene
Just not the thing to do.

I sit in the Dog Park, Bucky's walked
Will have to walk him home.
Then tend to my own life to live
And see what I can do.

I ate my first meal of the day
And drank my fill of coffee.
It changes not what I will do
Life simply goes along.

Some people come, some people go
That's change enough for me.
It's getting hot, then hotter still
It is a Yuma summer.

Today is Thursday, Bingo today
A lot of people go.
A past time many here enjoy
I'll take a pass today.

I'll take my lunch at noon today
Though many call it dinner.
And evening meal that they call dinner
For us, we call it supper.

A lunch for me comes in between
My breakfast and dinner at noon.
And dinner and supper in afternoon
That's called a lunch for me.

But who am I to buck the tide
The "Many!" set the tide.
A different path that gets us there
The end of another day.

Therese many people, many paths
We come from many places.
Yet live our lives in quiet peace
And look askance at them.

Life we live, our many lives
Perhaps it's like a puzzle?
Which one fits here, which one fits there?
We have the time to ponder.

So life, this life, that each one lives
Continues day by day.
With little order we survive
To live the life we live.

Glen Wasson
July 6, 2023

#775
Our Lives

Today I'm wondering about our lives
You live yours and I'll live mine.
But will we intersect in space
And play like bumper cars?

Our lives collide at a point in time!
A bit before or after
Would make the difference we each need
To go upon our ways.

Do I care where you are going
And how about you for me?
Do you really care where my life leads?
We're passing in the night.

Am I an iceberg in your life,
In which you crash and sink?
Or do we pass without a look
And simply go our way?

Sometimes that passing is meant to be
Hold out our hands and touch.
And touching leads to holding hands
And that may lead to hugs.

Do our lives have real meaning,
Or are they really chance?
Do we go the way of a pin-ball game,
Or do we have a choice?

Does a touch or a ring have real meaning to us
Or do we just pass them off?
"It's just by chance and I don't care!"
Oh, what we let go bye.

For those of us at Y.S.L.
We've mostly lived long lives.
Collected memories, each his own
We'll carry to the grave.

Unless we choose to share them out
With each and everyone.
Then our lives are known wide
And gain additional meaning.

That's why I write my poetry
My life's within my words.
Read them slowly, let them sink
And maybe some will click.

Share your thoughts with me today
Tomorrow we can be friends.
You know my life, I know yours
That way we'll both be richer.

Greetings to life, to both our lives
We both have thoughts to share.
With someone different every day
Our lives are mixed together.

Glen Wasson
July 6, 2023

#776
About Our Lives

This, my third poem for the day
I'm really questioning life.
Is it this or that or something else,
Or am I in left field?

Life has questions, many too,
To ponder and discuss.
Philosophers will question why
And then propose solutions.

We all live life in different ways
Are we gay or are we gloomy?
Do we smile or do we frown right now,
Or do we simply do?

"Life's a chore!" some people say
"What would you do if you were me?
Would you continue as you are
Or would you change your ways?"

Some lives are good, some lives are bad
And some from the pit of hell!
My life's not yours and yours not mine
We have to live our own.

We cannot change what life sends us
But can try to avoid it.
What's in your power, that's to do
To do, not bellyache.

So live your life as best you can
Excel in all you do.
Life's not a treat, you must live yours
You have to make a choice.

Look at your neighbors across the way,
How are they living life?
If they are happy, follow them
Choose the right way, right now.

I know life's not really fair to us
Some get the short end of life.
So get the most of what you get
And enter Senior life.

This is what we've all worked for
Time to retire, relax.
Life as we've never seen before
Who knew it'd be this hard.

Old age is what we're living now
It aint like life before.
It comes with aches and pains galore,
Welcome to Golden Age.

Glen Wasson
July 6, 2023

#777
Good or Bad

Do you need to feel sorrow to really feel glad?
Can we assume one without experiencing the other?
How do we know what is good or is bad?
Is it natural to lean toward the one or the other?

Do we naturally know what is good or is bad,
What is happy and gay or just wasting away?
Dare we try to rely on whatever we know?
Do we know what it is to have known before?

Life without knowing is life without cause!
Life without cause, cause there's nothing to know!
To know what we know is knowledge indeed!
Knowledge and knowing, not really the same!

If we know nothing, yes nothing at all,
Are we ignorant smart or ignorant dumb?
Does a wise one admit he knows nothing at all
Or seek knowledge a bit to be smarter than all?

If I think I am smarter than you think you are,
Who will judge us a winner and how will he judge?
Are there books we can read to test out our smarts?
Dare a human decide what is knowledge to him?

Am I greater than great if I'm smarter than all?
Do I sit high above in a chair above all?
Do I rule over you, do you do what I say?
Should we hold an election to settle it all?

Glen Wasson
July 9, 2023

#778
Freedom

I've wanted for a while, I have
To write about our Freedoms.
The Freedoms that we have right here
In the Good Old U.S.A.

When did it come and was it free
And do we all deserve it?
Why do we fly the flag so high
Take pause, and then salute it?

Those foreign to our shores, they wonder
Why we are so proud of flag and land?
And sing it's praises all day long
And shoot the fireworks high.

Twas not the same back in the time
We were a part of England.
But had no say in what they did
Were only told--"Obey!"

Without a "Word" the "Taxes" hurt,
We did rebel a bit.
We threw some tea into the sea
Though costumed as some others.

We took a stand upon a bridge
We lost some good men there.
The Crown sent men to put us down
The line must have been drawn.

Did not start out to fight a war
We mostly made a statement.
But met a brick wall with the Crown
We did what needed done.

So now we hold the flag up high
On buildings short and tall,
In parks, on schools and homes throughout the land!
It fly's because we're free.

We're proud of what we have become
A Country far and wide.
We must be doing something right
They come here by the millions!

So Proudly fly the flag today
Stand tall and pause, salute.
It stands for all of those who fought
Back then and yet today.

Glen Wasson
July 10, 2023

#779
"The Day"

How are we to address the Day,
Is it "Sir," "Miss," or "Madam?"
Or is it not a person at all,
But a thing to be only observed?

For many of us, we greet in the morn
At a time when it's new to us.
We toast it with coffee, perhaps with cream
Preparing to go forth with zest.

But for some the night was later than yours
The sun has risen a bit more by then.
It may take two cups to get us to move
Forget even asking for cream.

Not everyone rises when we think they should
We all know the proper old time.
"Time is money," "Sunshine's wasting," come on now get going.
"Lazy bones," you may have been called, "There's plenty of work
to be done."

Ever work the mid-night shift
When it's dark and nobodies out?
You get the crap to do at night
That nobody else will do.

The second shift is a compromise
Still get to sleep at night.
Miss out on all the happy hours
And other normal stuff.

We mostly like the normal way
Get up, go work, go home.
When that schedule gets upset
We stumble or we fall.

I've worked them all and made it work
Not always by my choice.
I had a boss who spied on me
And then he chewed me out.

Sometimes you have to work the odd
They pay you more to do it.
But then you're a slave to the cash you make
Must learn to just get by.

I've had my morning cup of joe
I had three cups at noon.
I finished off with three tonight
And now it's time to rest.

The morning sun will come too soon
And I will have to do what's right.
An early riser? Morning sun?
Or do it all mid-morn.

Address the day as best you can,
It's something we must do.
That's why we live but eighty years,
Too many more would kill us.

Glen Wasson
July 10, 2023

#780
Prose and Poetry

Why cry because you are hurt,
Are you hurt or just offended?
Tears come easily in these modern days,
Can we not stand up, be firm?

Of the prose that just drones on,
Some sentences complete,
Where is the poem in all those words?
Where is the flavor and spice?

Use the spice that makes a poem
That gives it flavor and smell.
Anyone can serve a bland, bland meal,
Anyone can write some words.

If writing prose write prose.
Don't pass it off as poetry.
Where are the brushes and paints you use
To paint a picture of words?

Do the strokes flow and swirl,
Do the colors stand and shout?
Does the canvas come to life
Just as a page of words?

I have a voice and words that cut
Like a sword of old would do.
How we bring them to life today
Is our use of vocabulary.

As a poet we use words not paint
But still we leave a picture.
We still must leave a view of life
To answer the questions it brings.

Not everyone desires to read
Of prose and poetry.
Though both may paint a picture clear
And satisfy your thoughts.

As a person we must ask
What else of life there is?
Desire to leave a legacy
For someone else to read.

With the minds we have we still go forth
Facing life with hope.
Hope to grow in mind and heart,
Be better than we were.

So grow my people, stand and rise
Be tall and lead the way.
Show everyone what life can be
That life that we must live.

Glen Wasson
July 12, 2023

#781
A Day in Life

The sun is setting in the west
The evening is coming on.
The day's been made of what it was
Will have to search it through.

Moments come, moments go
Days begin and end.
Tomorrow will bring another try
To live a perfect life.

What is meant, "A perfect life?"
Is it even possible?
Do we search and search to make it be
Or simply let it come?

Could be a struggle all one's life
Pursuing what we want.
Life that's still a step away
May never be in reach.

As the sun never ceases it's voyage in the sky
Will life ever come into reach?
May we ever believe that we may grasp the ring
And win the prize of life.

Is life worth the effort that's required to make it real
Or is there a simpler, easier way?
Confusing as life is we still must work through
To live all this life to the very last bit.

Glen Wasson
July 13, 2023

#782
My Poems

Have spent some time just reading poems,
Poems I wrote back then.
A few weeks back, some months ago
Even a year or two.

I even now amaze myself
They're not too bad to read.
They speak of life and how we live
I think they're worth a read.

Am I too proud to say they're good
Am I pompous to speak that way?
They are written from the deep within
Expressing how I feel.

Have to share them, get them out
Let others know how I feel.
I have one book, one hundred poems
Another soon will be.

I want to share my many thoughts,
My hopes and my desires.
The near eight hundred my journals have
Four volumes on my desk.

I now am printing little books
Of twelve or sixteen pages.
I print and fold and staple them
The total now is twelve.

These little books I'd like to sell
Have found one store to place.
With others in my mind to try
Will I be disappointed?

These little books are more than poems
There's history and how-to.
Again they're from my mind and soul
Handcrafted with some passion.

So pick one up, just a few bucks
Will make an old man happy.
I hope your face will gain a smile
Already one on mine

Glen Wasson
July 17, 2023

#1   Poems of the Courtyard in Yuma
#2   My Life and the Weather in Yuma
#3   Yuma Senior Living
#4   Philosophy
#5   A Poetry Sampler
#6   Sadness and Grief
#7   What is Poetry
#8   A Do-It-Yourself Chapbook (in progress)
#9   The Spice of Poetry
#10 Tiny Poems By 24
#11 Four Long Poems
#12 A Snippet of The History of Yuma, Arizona

#783
Heat

There's wispy clouds up in the sky
Up there in all the blue.
They go in different ways up there
The wind up there is moving.

Don't feel it here, down on the ground
It's quiet, getting hot.
Should be above one-ten today
Our summer has arrived.

The extreme heat has come to stay,
Will see a lot like this.
And yet we stay year after year
Luxuriate in winter.

With A.C. it is not so bad
Not like the days of old.
Yet some will suffer from the heat
And even need some help.

Outsiders often ask of us
"Why do you stay down here?"
When acclimated, used to it,
It's just a part of life.

Don't see the snow or icy roads,
Don't wear those winter clothes.
Snow shovels never come of use
Umbrellas just for shade.

Yes, there's reasons we stay here,
This Yuma we call home.
We have most everything we need
We like our little town.

The Freeway travels East and West
Cities three hours away.
Most people traveling through don't stay,
And we can hardly blame them.

I look through glass and see the heat
While sitting on the couch.
With air that's cooled to seventy-four,
One-fourteen outside today.

My shoes are off, my feet are up,
Had breakfast, walked the dog.
Writing poems that come to mind,
Enjoying senior life.

I have long pants, a heavy coat
For when it does get cold.
But shorts, tee shirts, mostly works
That's why we're here in Yuma.

Glen Wasson
July 18, 2023

#784
Mexicali Rose

Mexicali Rose from 1938
A song that I remember dear.
From the mid 1940's
A song we used to dance too.

Made popular in a movie by Gene Autry
Before the war hit home in '41.
After the war we moved to California
The family often gathered for a dance.

I miss those days, so happy
Family all around.
Together often for a weekend
At someones home together.

After four years of war
The peace was good to have.
Rations were over, goods were here
Travel was free to do.

As I look back some seventy years
So very few are left.
Memories bring tears to eyes
Never coming back.

Just found the song on the internet
From eighty-three years ago.
A movie clip saved for this time
Brought back the memories.

Glen Wasson
May 26, 2021

#785
Dog Park

Should we let our dogs bark at the dog park
When they're running within the fence?
Like someone walks by, a stranger to them,
No way they can do them harm.

They chase along the fence and bark
Sound fierce, but heed not "Stop!"
It's like some people they don't like
We really are not in control.

For the most part they are happy and gentle
They just need to run, poop and pee.
And then upon a seldom time
They exercise their bark.

Glen Wasson
July 22, 2023

#786
Ignored

Hard to take, to be ignored
To be not thought of by them.
Why do they do that—and not call
It only needs a bit.

Is it too much to ask of them
To call and chat a bit?
Return a message that I left,
Of course they have a life.

We're spread apart by many miles
And Time Zones come between.
There's thirty—forty years time too
We all are all so different.

But still it hurts to be alone
From family far and wide.
Will they miss me when I'm gone
Or will they carry on?

There is so much that I have done
That I would like to share.
Done this, done that, I bounce with joy
But this I cannot share.

Was not at their most needed times
Was not the Dad they needed.
Was off there working somewhere else
Not always at their home.

I have Michelle and that is good
She keeps me leveled out.
But she gets calls most every day
Fulfilled by friends I lack.

Admittedly I'm lonely now
I miss my four grown kids.
I wish they'd call and say hello
Before I have to cry.

Glen Wasson
July 22, 2023

#787
More of Life

Dare we fear things life brings to us
Or simply disregard?
Are we brave enough to stumble on
And make a life for us?

Life is not a simple thing
It must be fought to win.
Is not for weak or feeble ones
It's for the brave and strong.

The weak and feeble will survive
Just like a lot of others.
But will miss out the joy that comes
From fighting the good fight.

You cannot fight without a scratch
And often worse than that.
Cuts and wounds are common place
The fight is fought with blood.

Some fear the fight and slink away
Even to hide out.
Afraid to face what must faced
And stand up to the world.

While others get up off the ground
Pick up their sword and fight.
They stand up to adversity
And struggle on to win.

Life is like a battlefield
There's winners and there's losers.
The ground is rough, not even at all
The fight's not always fair.

Some have the high ground, looking down
For others, all uphill.
Some swords are sharper, better honed
And others dull and short.

Such is the life we all must face
Some get the easy way.
While others have to fight and claw
For every inch they gain.

Winners and losers, success, defeat
Will be there to the end.
Not always to select and choose
But what life gives to us.

We may not win but still succeed
By how we choose to fight.
Some are down but not defeated
They still will stand erect.

Choose the way that you will fight
It may be to the end.
Each one is judged by how they strive
Desire is all that's seen.

Glen Wasson
July 26, 2023

#788
The Loneliest Time Of Day

The son is setting in the west
The night is almost here.
It's winter, snow is on the ground
My hands and feet are cold.

I'm tramping through the edge of town
I've crossed the tracks divide.
The lights are dimmer where they live
Sometimes a bulb hangs down.

The loneliness is hard to take
There's no one out, about.
I am alone, they're all inside
Around a stove for warmth.

Icicles hang from off the roof
They make it even colder.
The snow's not quite a foot in depth
But drags upon my feet.

Been out, about, my day's bout done
Will soon be heading home.
Don't wish for other days like this
This one's been quite enough.

Glen Wasson
July 28, 2023

#789
I'm Wearing a Hat

I'm wearing a hat today, I am
To shield my head from the sun
It's hot and bright out there today
Don't want to get a burn.

Don't have much hair upon my head
Some say that I am bald.
I'd rather say "Outgrew my hair!"
I'm still a little vane.

Don't have a place to lay it down
When in the dining room.
Will have to leave it on my head
Though may be called "Improper."

I got my hat when I got my boots
With shirts and pants—ensemble.
I sort of like my western look
It makes me look dressed up.

Will have to wear it oftener
To make a fashion statement.
Already people look at me
Some even shake their heads.

"I am what I am!" as Popeye said
Can pick me out of a crowd.
Will always be a bit of a kind
That goes his own sweet way.

Glen Wasson
July 28, 2023

#790
Life Philosophy

We all are part of life right now
We're living, thus we are.
Can't simply say "I'm out of here!"
And kiss this life away.

Would be so easy if we could
So easy to get out.
But you would have to end it all
To stop all that you are.

To end it all would be one way
But what would you achieve?
Might enter in an afterlife
That you would not enjoy.

Life was never promised "Good!"
There's good, there's bad, there's ugly.
What ere you have may be your choice
Ever think of that?

Somewhere within this world we live
There's lucky, and not so.
There's blessed and unblessed, not the same
We all are something different.

So look around and see the world
The world as it really is.
Go choose what ere is your desire
Don't blame it on the others.

Glen Wasson
August 2, 2023

#791
Drum Major

We always want to be out front
To lead and never follow.
To be the one who's in control
And not the one controlled.

The leader always looks the best
The uniform most noticed.
A mace in hand is long and bright
So everyone can see.

In charge of all who follow them
They are a stately figure.
Alone, out front, they lead the band
And all behind will follow.

There's only one can count the beat
It must be done alone.
There's only one who's in control
Can be no second leader.

Not everyone can be that one
Though everyone partakes.
The only sound the leader makes
The shrill sound of the whistle.

It's not a post that's in demand
Not everyone pursues it.
You are responsible for all
And cannot shrug it off.

The strutting major out in front
Must understand who follow.
While in control, can't discipline
Must bring them all together.

Is this the call you wish to take
To stand and seek the glory?
Standing out front, it's lonely there
No one to left or right.

When all goes wrong, the beat is lost,
Guess who receives the blame?
It's not the drummer in the back
It's they who stand out front.

Though one may lead a hundred fold
It's not all vain and glory.
But when the band is playing great
The biggest smile is yours.

Glen Wasson
August 4, 2023

#792
The Coffee Bean

I read some poems the other night
At the Good Old Coffee Bean.
I joined a group of eight or nine
To play and sing and read.

Lots of strings to pluck and strum
The mic was always on.
The lyrics of the songs went on
To tapping toes and feet.

The coffee drinks went on to flow
And wet the persons whistle.
Kept all of us alert and bold
To clap for those up front.

An easy crowd, they clapped for all
No angry words were said.
Were happy for all those who came
A happy group it was.

Some customers would come and go
Not really interfering.
They might have wondered what was up
To view a group like us.

It only happens twice a month
The first and third last days.
You come, sign up and get a drink
And wait your turn to play

Glen Wasson
August 6, 2023

#793
Union

I have no hair, I have no teeth
But still I have two feet.
They help me stand up straight and tall
For my land—America.

The Constitution compromised
To bring them all together.
It had it's faults, as all things do
But formed--"More Perfect Union."

More Perfect—than what came before
More-so than what they knew.
It was the best that they could do
With what they had to work.

Some had slaves and some did not
That was a fact of life.
They must have had more different ways
That they must overcome.

Though it was not perfect
It's worked out pretty well.
We fought a war to keep it one
And now we number fifty.

Our Countries built on give and take
Not everyone agrees.
But in the end we must accept
Our Not So Perfect Union.

Glen Wasson
August 7, 2023

#794
Wisdom

Walking and talking with others is nice
Bonding of minds as we rest in our joy.
Without interaction with others we are
One lonely person whose thoughts are his own.

A Hermite or guru may live all alone
Considered a wise one by many he sees.
His thoughts are his own, not invaded by ours
Is he wise or just different—what sets him apart?

If we say we are different and go live alone
Will they think more of us than they would have before?
Do we sit and just mumble and say crazy things
Are we better of mind than the ones who are nuts?

If we bend at the waist and make use of a cane
And let our hair grow and not wash it at all,
Wear camel hair coats and no sandals at all,
Our smell may be different but will it be wise?

Most of us want to be thought of as wise
But what must we do to secure what we want?
Leaving our life in the town or the farm
Leaving our loved ones to fend on their own.

Perhaps being wise is not what we just thought
Perhaps being normal is O.K. to be.
And clean and respectful is also O.K.
Sounds better to me than to live in a cave.

So wise and good living may lead one to be
At a level of wisdom that others may see.
They may seek you out and may show you respect
An honor you've earned in the midst of a crowd.

Be honest in wisdom you have in your head
Treat others with kindness and do good to all.
They have their own wisdom that you may admire.
Rejoice that you have what the others pursue.

Glen Wasson
August 13, 2023

#795
Here's How
Hurricane Hillary
Hits Home – 2023

Alliteration – Check it out.

It's August 20, 23
In Yuma's Monsoon season.
A storm to beat all storms before
They say will be here soon.

The rain came through a bit last night
As well as yesterday.
Today we're left with just the wind
It's gusty, high and wild.

If laying loose it blows around
Leaves, paper and dust.
The worst I've seen since I've been here
The twenty-three years I've been.

They say we'll get a three inch rain
Don't know if we have yet.
But winds enough to blow things round
Will be a mess tomorrow.

Inside it's a gentle, quiet sound
Of wind that blows outside.
The trees blow wildly in the wind
So much you'd think they'd break.

I sort-of like to sit outside
And feel the wind blow through.
I watch the trees whip back and forth
Like fighting for their lives.

The birds, they suffer in this wind
The branches up and down.
It's not a peaceful time for them
Their home is not secure.

I'll spend the day at home today
And write this simple poem.
And try to think of what was like
Back in the early days.

Our forecast said "It's coming soon!"
We had time to prepare.
For them it was "It's here today!"
All hell was bursting forth.

Don't think it'll be here very long
Before the winds die down.
Tomorrow will be a better day
At least I hope will be.

Is this the worst that we will face?
If so I'm glad it's so.
While I am safe, others will fear
Of what the storm has brought.

Must take the bad that comes with good
Not any we control.
We'll leave it to a higher power
Controlling all of that.

Glen Wasson
August 20, 2023

#796
Clouds Up High

Sometimes I miss the clouds up high,
The ones that dot the sky.
Like puff balls in the blue so blue,
They float so soft and easy.

The Yuma sky is mostly blue
The clouds are few and far.
Don't see the shape of animals
That charge the mind to think.

Rain clouds are something we don't see
But every once a while.
There's contrails lining west to east
But they're not really clouds.

For many people clouds are real,
They see them every day.
Even have the thunder clouds
In colors green and gray.

We have twelve months a year to grow
The crops we grow so well.
Can all be done without a cloud
The river brings the water.

We do get rain from rain clouds gray
About three inches per.
Spread out over a year of months
You might say it is dry.

Remember back when I was young,
Some twenty years or more.
Lived in the great mid-west back east,
Saw clouds most every day.

Looked up and saw a dog or cat
A dragon or a boat.
Could always find something to see
Might have to squint a bit.

No days like that in Yuma town,
Are few and far between.
Just blue and blue, that boring blue,
Without a cloud in sight.

Glen Wasson
August 24, 2023

#797
Pigeons

I think the pigeon has a bum rap
Because of how he lives.
Most others nest in bush or trees
But pigeons on your house.

They fly so high and land on top
Of buildings far and wide.
And leave their droppings where we live
Because we live so close.

Why don't they live as nature wants
In natures vast domain?
Why must they live right where I do
Like an unwanted guest?

They really are a gorgeous bird
So sleek and proud they walk.
And in the air they are the king
Of all the city birds.

The smaller birds they move so fast
Their here, their there, their gone.
But pigeons strut in slow proud steps
As if they own the place.

They're big enough, we see their size
Their wings, their heads, their bodies.
They earn their place within our realm
To simply watch them fly.

There's larger birds with grace to show
But don't live in our cities.
They dwell where natures rough and real
Out in the great beyond.

Eagles and such are truly king
But rarely venture in.
The prey they seek is large and wild
Not present in our town.

So pigeons are what most we see
They're neighbors to us all.
We know just where they're resting now
By looking on the ground.

Glen Wasson
August 25, 2023

#798
Duffy MacDowel

We're standing here in the midst of the day
And talking 'bout Duffy MacDowel.
A man with two fists, but a heart made of gold
And an eye for the ladies to boot.

Would not say he's kind, he's different than that
He's gruff and he's rough and he's tough.
He's not what he was when younger he was
But he's made it this long in his life.

There's a scar on the left and a gash on the right
And his face is not what you'd call clean.
But he smiles with a grin that reveals a tooth gap
And there's hair on his chinny, chin, chin.

The towns not large where Duffy's come from
And it shows that he's been round the block.
He's met quite some men who are not thought as nice
And he's sat and he's drank through the night.

If you buy him a pint he will be your's tonight
And he'll sing and drink ales with the best.
Tomorrow he'll be round whether you are or not
He always looks for a friend.

At home is his wife and she cleans and she cooks
And she cleans other houses for pay.
While he sits and he drinks and he watches the telly
With never a care to his name.

With a cue in his left and some darts in his right
He's the steady of any proud pub.
Keep his glass full and he'll play at his best
And flirt with the girl at the bar.

On the pitch it is known that he knows his way round
How to dribble and kick with the best.
And as for the rules he has broken a few
And even a Red Card or two.

Near where he calls home, a canal that he knows
As he visits it more than he'd like.
But when he is drunk the cold water feels good
As he seeks the warm hug of his wife.

She's not always happy to see him come home
When it's one or it's two in the morn.
They may argue a bit but by dawn it's alright
And they'll kiss and make up once again.

So this is the life of one Duffy MacDowel
Though not perfect he's still quite a man.
He's always a friend till his anger's aroused
After all, he's Duffy MacDowel.

Glen Wasson
August 25, 2023

A take on Andy Capp – comic

#799
HOT!

It's Sunday afternoon and HOT!
About one hundred twelve.
It could go up a point or two
But feels good in the shade.

A slight breeze blows, it does feel nice
The afternoon is quiet.
Seems like nothing wants to move
Just lie there and relax.

The sky is cloudless, none at all
Just a blue, so blue, blue sky.
Even birds choose not to fly
In this Hot! Hot! afternoon.

I ate my lunch, then chose to rest
I sat down in a glider.
And gazed upon a garden green
With water trickling down.

We live in Yuma, in A.Z.
Down in the southwest point.
It's desert any way you go
We are a garden spot.

Another month, will start to cool
And Snowbirds will arrive.
They come for five, six months at most
Then back to Northern climes.

Don't venture very far out there
A few miles out and back.
But know the fields are green with crops
The harvest soon will be.

The River flows right by the town
It brings us all our water.
Provides for all the crops we grow
And all we drink to boot.

Some go to cool their bodies off
They float and swim—relax.
It's one way to suppress the heat
And wait for cooler weather.

Some-days I wonder why I'm here
Where no one wants to be.
This little bit of Yuma town
The place that I call home.

Glen Wasson
August 27, 2023

#803
Kaboom!

Kaboom! Went the thunder, in the middle of the night
I missed if there was lightning.
The rain was hitting on the window pane
The start of something strange.

We're Yuma people here, no rain
Except from time to time.
I saw it back, 2000 year
The streets were running full.

They call it Monsoon time for us
The air is humid, hot.
We get some showers, wind and dust
But nothing quite like this.

It poured today, that's right it poured
You might say cats and dogs.
The walks were deep with what fell down
And sand bags were set out.

I made it down to lunch O.K.
Was just a little cloudy.
But during lunch it all broke loose
It really poured right down.

Those inside left raincoats home
And now they wish they hadn't.
It's running off the roof in sheets
Noway to get in dry.

And now, just two hours after that
The sun is coming out.
There still are clouds up in the sky
Maybe they'll blow away.

Perhaps we're spoil't in Yuma town
Hardly see the rain.
But we made up for it today
A lot of rain fell down.

Out in the desert, gullies run
Full of dirt and water.
Overflows the road below
And sweeps away the cars.

They tell you not to drive through that
When running water flows.
But people never listen close
And do it anyway.

I hope this does it for this year
Two hours full of rain.
We're not prepared for this out here
Out here in Yuma town.

Glen Wasson
September 2, 2023

#804
Poetry

Been reading books 'bout poetry
Then read some of my own.
I feel good 'bout what I wrote
It's really not so bad.

I have a way of using words
In ways that might seem strange.
But gets the word out that I want
To make them reminisce.

I like that I can take them back
To when times were so different.
Remember times both good and bad
That makes up all their lives.

I read my poems on Saturday night
At the place—The Coffee Bean.
It's open mic for all to rise
And share with all the world.

We have ten minutes to get it out
A song, a tune, a poem.
For some it's new and hard to do
For others, it's old hand.

Most are brave, but some are shy
They look out, see a crowd.
But stand their place before the mic
And let it all come out.

We all have something, want to share
This here's where you can do it.
Come in, sign up, and then sit down
And wait until your turn.

I'm glad that some can appreciate
The poems I write and read.
To share what wells up from below
Means all the world to me.

Glen Wasson
September 4, 2023

#805
Morning to Noon

Oh, the thoughts that come to mind
When Morning turns to Noon.
The Sun is rising high above
The heat is building too.

The Morning didn't 'mount to much
I mostly passed it off.
I ate some, slept some, read some more
And now I raise my pen.

I thought about what I should write
Yet nothing came to mind.
So this is what I'm writing 'bout
What ever enters now.

The words they come, they seem to flow
They're easy to write down.
Enjoy the mindfull words that come
As such a time as this.

I've read some paper, read a book
And now I'm writing down,
My thoughts that come to mind today,
The joy that comes to me.

It's such a life that I enjoy
The one I live alone.
But then I get to share it all,
I give it to the world.

Glen Wasson
September 10, 2023

#806
Writing in Three Quarter Meter

I'm trying a new type of writing I am
To try and see if it will work.
I usually write in a four meter way
Now trying to change it a bit.

But here I am back to my old way of script
Can't help it, it's just what I do.
But notice it's 1-2-3, waltz time for sure
And I can't stop going even if I could.

The meter is in me I can't get it out
Must do it again and again.
It's driving me crazy, I can't make it stop
I think I will just need to end.

Glen Wasson
September 10, 2023

#807
Marching

I fell in place, a line of marching men.
They march to find a war in which to fight.
Their leaders bravely lead them into war
Ambivalent to fears these men may have.

Marching! Marching! Left, right, left!
The men have fit their pace to match the count.
When will this marching end and give them rest?
The end of day draws nigh, it must be soon.

Is man destined to march right into war?
The peace we seek is always far away.
It may be possible to sheath the sword
And spare the bloodshed that is due to be.

The halt is called, the men are put at ease,
This is the time to take a drink or two.
And rest the legs that marched throughout the day
And rest the weary body they support.

They pitch a tent, a shelter made for two,
And start a fire to cook their evening meal.
They wash the grime collected off their face
Prepare to rest the night in solitude.

The moon is up, the stars are out, it's night,
Another day of marching they will face.
But that's tomorrow, tonight's a time to rest,
And when it comes they'll give it all their best.

Glen Wasson
September 12, 2023

#808
A Poem of Beats

Once in a while, in the Land of Toad
There happens a moment of happy glee.
It causes a person to laugh or cry
Depending on your point of view.

The meter is simple, it's 1,2,3,4,
Your counting the beats and that's what you must do.
It may not make sense to a yet untrained ear
But that's just the way that it is.

The Land of Toad is a fairy-book land
In a land that we'd call make-believe.
But it marches along with the beat of the best
And continues to not sound sing-song.

It doesn't make sense as a poem should have been
But it marches along still the same.
Do we care if it's stupid, it still fits the beat
So it sounds sort of O.K. to me.

We now see how easy a poem comes to life
It doesn't take much skill at all.
Just stumble along with a beat in your mind
And it all comes along as it should.

Here's to the poem that I now just wrote down
Without any thoughts that it should.
So I end it right here, before it gets lost
And call it a poem above poems.

Glen Wasson
September 14, 2023

#809
Dreaming Poems

I sit and look up in the sky
To see if there are clouds?
They're not within my line of sight
But may be to my back.

A building tall is at my back
I cannot see behind.
But in the sky that I can see
It's just clear sky to me.

Here in Yuma clouds are few
The sky is mostly clear.
So many days to fly their planes
And practice what they do.

While I don't fly I drive a lot
Don't want to see a storm.
With winds and rains I don't care for
Would rather it be clear.

We've had Monsoon a time or two
Don't really care for them.
They hassle things, upset the roads
Not help to anyone.

When dreaming poems I sit outside
And wiggle words around.
Then come inside to write them down
And finally type them in.

Glen Wasson
September 14, 2023

#810
A Poem in Trimeter

He slept through breakfast and lunch
And through the supper that came.
Is he tired or simply lazy?
Maybe he just likes to sleep.

He is, after-all, an old man
Free to do what he pleases to do.
The beat of his drum is slow
And answers to no one but self.

Why would anyone question
His motives or even desire.
If he chooses to sleep, so be it
It's a life he has chosen for him.

Some say, "Let lying dogs lie."
They're happy just as they are.
As we age we also get lazy,
With old age we garner respect.

Now he's up writing poems in his journal
Out of bed to do just that.
When the desire o'rtakes him
His body comes to life.

If desire is what stimulates him
Let it be, let it be, let it be.
Works better than prodding his body
Or nagging his feeble old brain.

Glen Wasson
September 18, 2023

#811
Desire and Effort

How humble is the one who writes in search of fame and
glory.
Should he be proud or hang his head and wait for fame to
come?
A writers goal is words wrote down, not thoughts left in
his head.
Without the pen and words wrote down the paper stays all
white.

And so is life to many men, they try but don't succeed.
Is effort by it's-self enough, does passion enter in?
Desire and drive are needed too to make the effort work.
Such is life to one like me, we get up, go to work.

Sometimes I want to stay in bed, to rest and dream a bit.
But drive removes me from my bed and gets me up to
write.
It only takes a word or phrase to start the words to flow
I really don't have full control but must respond and
write.

Do others have the same desire to get up and to go?
The bed is warm and comfortable, so nice to stay and rest.
But duty calls, the bugle sounds and we must rise,
respond.
Such is life to a driven one, get up, go forth and fight.

It isn't something you turn off but only respond to.
Desire and effort, added up, may find the fame and glory.
Stand up and spread your arms out wide and reach out for
the stars.
The goal is what makes it worthwhile, a goal that you
have reached.

Glen Wasson
September 19, 2023

#813
Clouds

The clouds are puffy in the sky
Above the town of Yuma.
They're puffy—fluffy--floaty too
Not often seen in Yuma.

The sky is blue, as it should be
The clouds are what is new.
They are a welcome sight to me
Don't see them everyday.

They make no sound as they float up there
They scarcely move at all.
Saw many when I lived back East
Back East in Wichita.

It's warm as I sit and look above,
Another perfect day.
Shirtsleeves and shorts are all I wear
No need for greater things.

But this is Yuma, where I live
A warm and sunny day.
That's why I live here all year round
For days that are so perfect.

Glen Wasson
September 21, 2023

#814
Waiting for a Video to Load

We all know how fast computers are,
It's just a click and—now.
So why am I writing a poem in my journal book
While waiting for a video to load?

It's 60%, 12 minutes to go
It seems like it is slow.
I need to learn to open two files.
Is that too much to ask?

I'm new to YouTube, my first time
To try to add some content.
First fifty are trash or so they say
So forty-nine to go.

Glen Wasson
September 21, 2023

#816
He Takes Me to the Dog Park – by Bucky

He takes me to the dog park
So I go one and two.
He does it cause he loves me
Or so I have been told.

He's married to my Mama
The one who saved me from
The pound, the shelter I came from,
She rescued me from there.

And yes he loves me, this I know
Because he's always there
To take me down each morning time
Although he may be late.

I hold it in as I am young
I only didn't once.
It wasn't wet, was just a pile
That easily got picked up.

He likes to play a game with me
He teases me a lot.
He says "Let's go!" then doesn't go,
I run both back and forth.

He likes to see me run about
To send me back and forth
I like to think it's a game we play
In prep of going down.

We are two males with one female
She chose us both in time.
But I am #1 I think
She chose me first I know.

The three of us sleep on the bed
They cover up—I don't.
They kick me off from time to time
Sometimes I just get off.

We have a nice house, they feed me too
And give me water to drink.

I ran off once to chase a cat
She caught me in the street.
I'm not street smart, you know what I mean
Now keeps me on a leash.

That's about all I've got to say
About the man called Glen.
We go forth, once a day we do
I hope we keep it up.

Glen Wasson
September 27, 2023

#817
One Week

It's been a week since they took me away
On a gangly, shiny, gurney.
They strapped me on and covered up
And smoothly rolled me out.

Two trips I made that weekend
The first was at midnight.
They brought me home at five A.M.
Said shakes would soon pass on.

Bout two P.M. fell off the bed
My back hit on nightstand.
But when I'm down I can't get up
So called the Med Tech Room.

Care person came and by herself
She got me on my feet.
When they got here they did they're job
And called the ambulance.

This time out I met some friends
And waved and called their names.
Again we went to the E.R.
This time they knew my name.

Some news arrived from morning trip
I had a new infection.
They drew some blood and found a room
And moved to 501.

Five days I spent in 501
Drew lots and lots of blood.
Needing to find when infection ends
And then one extra time.

Was not allowed to stand or walk
Without some one to hold.
Finally got to sit in chair
And watch the lone T.V.

Friday moved to Life Care home
To room 212A.
Rehab to be a week or two
Or less if it works out.

I now am hoping for Thursday morn
To leave here and go home.
The same day Shell has her teeth pulled out
Hope Bucky makes it through.

Tis Monday morn, October nine
We start another week.
Would like to go home Wednesday day
And join Michelle in life renewed.

Glen Wasson
October 9, 2023

#818
Another View of Life

Been reading poetry of old
They often speak of gloom and doom.
How life gets old and soul is lost
That's not my way of feeling.

For reasons known but to me
I look at life and notice glee!
I'm eighty-four and had a life
But still I'm looking forward.

In Yuma town the sky is blue
With few if any clouds.
I like it here, I'm comfortable
The heat I feel is warm.

Each day is new to me and so
I look with expectation.
What can I do today—what's new
Another poem I write.

Life is good to me, it is
It's left me with few scars.
Looking forward, not the back
I have a life to live.

Glen Wasson
October 9, 2023

#819
The Window

The window's bright, the sky is blue, the roof is lightly pink.
I gaze outside to see the world and that is what I see.
It's Monday afternoon right now and moving on toward eve.
I'm sitting in a black wheelchair and thinking bout the world.

Blank verse is what I'm writing in, that's rhythm without rhyme.
There are seven beats per line right now, no more, no less, just seven.
I like to play with words like this and see how they come out.
Words are tools that poets use to get their thoughts put down.

To some degree each line of seven could really be four—three.
That is my usual form to use but this is fun to do.
Some like a song they can sing along with and others tap their feet.
Some like a car that is big and long while others one that's fast.

Life is more than the window shows, there's more than that out there.
Air and space, sky and clouds, cars and people too.
I have an eye for joy and peace and relish life supreme.
Don't let the outside frighten you, stand firm as you are tall.

Can't get much done on your hands and knees, you must get up to work.
Life is work you can't relax, you must continue on.
Stand up to work and reach up high, the stars are high above.
Collect them till your quivers full and you're prepared to live.

Glen Wasson
October 9, 2023

#820
Together

Tis many days since I went away
Of our little place called home.
Where we joined our hands and joined our hearts
In love we hold so deep.

I miss my Shell, I miss you so
I want to be with you.
To hold your hand and hug you close
To feel your very being.

We sit apart, yet still are one
Each in our own small space.
We spend our time away and yet
We move to be together.
To touch and kiss and give a smile
And share a bit of time.

Today and tomorrow I'm given to be here
Then Friday coming home.
Don't know morn or afternoon
Will never be too soon.

That my dear is how I miss you
Your smile, your face, your touch.
I relish moments such as these
I want you close to me.

Glen Wasson
October 11, 2023

#821
Do I Miss You, Yes I Do

Do I miss you, yes I do.
I miss you more than words can say,
Your touch, your smile, your voice, your face
All mean so much to me.

Will be the most of two weeks Dear
Since I got wheeled away.
I've seen you once, it's been a while
I miss you every day.

I miss our little chats where we
Express our love to other.
In terms only we can say and do
There's lots more in our minds.

Oh, to sit upon the couch
And hold you close to me.
And squeeze that little belly fat
You know I love to squeeze.

Its Wednesday now, will be two days
Before we're back together.
Look out world we have a lot
Of catching up to do.

Glen Wasson
October 11, 2023

#822
Wild Thoughts

Who but me would know what I mean
When I say what I think that I mean?
Words are words that have to be lined
Up in ways that allow one to speak.

A series of words make up a long line
Or maybe a short line of words.
For me I can choose four lines in a bunch
And that's what's called a stanza.

I skip a line to separate one
Stanza from the rest.
As you can see a line means something
But must be taken in the context of four.

Thoughts and lines and words and such
Are part of what I have sought to write.
To put in lines and bits of thought
Must now be aliened by me.

Words alone don't make a line
And lines don't make a thought.
But thoughts must be set out in a way
That makes some sense to me.

Glen Wasson
October 19, 2023

#825
Life Beats

Oh, how to look at the life we now live
To look and wonder why?
Are we happy and gay or mad in a way
Can we march to the beat of the poem?

Life has a rhythm that marches on
A rhythm like your heartbeat.
A steady rhythm is easy to feel
Just follow the beat that you feel.

We look to the sky to find rhythm
The Stars, the Moon, the Sun.
We sleep through the night cause we know in the morn
The Sun will appear like clockwork.

We're counting the beats, one two, three four.
Like heartbeats we hear, da Dum, da Dum.
The universe has a pattern it's own
da Dum, da Dum, da Dum.

Follow the beats that your life gives to you
Follow the beats with joy.
The beat of your heart may follow the Sun
And lay out the beat of your life.

Glen Wasson
October 24, 2023

#826
Morning Coming Forth

Oh, what wonder drifting forth
To end the night and greet the morn.
To look for light far to the east
To start the day anew.

The coolness of the morn is felt
Before the warmth of day takes o'er.
Nature has not yet awoke
And never a word has yet been spoke.

Stillness still envelopes all
The time between the morn and night.
Awaiting the first glimpse of light
In that far eastern sky.

The blackness of the sky becomes
An orange or pink, but just a glow.
Nothing can stop the glow to grow
The weight of day rolls on.

The sky's aglow but still no sun
But now it cannot be denied.
The day is rolling, rolling on
The sun breaks the horizon.

Golden rays illuminate
The morning dew on grass so late.
The sun's so bright the night takes flight
The day has full begun.

The rays of the sun are warm to feel
The heat of the day will find it's time.
The globe that navigates our sky
Will rule the day it brings.

All nature is awakened now
The birds are singing, flying high.
The critters running to and fro
All sorts of life emerge.

This day has surely now begun
Continue till the evening comes.
To blacken all the sky so blue
And start the cycle all anew.

Glen Wasson
October 25, 2023

#827
What Life is all About

What are we to figure out
What life is all about.
The how, the why, the where, the when
The things we wonder 'bout.

What is life but questions asked
The thoughts that flood the mind.
All those whys and where's and when's
Are we to even know?

I believe we humans were
Endowed with thoughts and mind.
To ponder all that does surround
This person I call me.

Most animals live out their life
With fear and sex and hunger.
They never have to wonder why
Or think about tomorrow.

Is it a privilege or curse
That we have all this knowledge.
Sometimes we only want to rest
And let the world go by.

Does Mama Deer have this to ponder
Or can they truly rest in peace?
With knowledge comes the need to care
Again, is this a curse?

So thoughts and words and deeds
It's not all just in our head.
We are a being, blest o're all
We rest on top the heap.

With all of that – responsible
Responsible for all.
They aren't there just to serve us all
But here for us to use.

To use we need to care for all
Responsible to care.
All nature we must care – protect
To make it last for all.

Do I mean to say that we have failed
To do what we should do?
To care for all we have in hand
To care for all we're given.

It's not too late to change our ways
And learn respect for nature.
Respect for all that's given us
Respect for who we are.

Glen Wasson
October 28, 2023

#828
Editing

I have been asked if I would dare
To edit what I've written?
To change a word, a line or phrase
Or move a thought about.

For most part NO! I'm satisfied
With what I've put on paper.
I write my thoughts as come to me
To change would be a lie.

My thoughts are on the page right now
From heart and mind and soul.
May change a tense or syllable
But mostly leave the same.

A thought may simply come to mind
Like this one did to me.
I had to stop, pick up the pen
And start another poem.

Sometimes I can't say what I mean
Without the pen and paper.
In four line Quatrains, 4 – 3 meter
Can write away my thoughts.

So why should I change anything
Would change the way I think.
Will stay with what is tried and true
It's brought me all this way.

Glen Wasson
October 28, 2023

#830
How I Write My Poems

I'm often asked how I write my Poems
How they come into my mind.
I often start with just one Line
And settle on a Meter.

With music in my heart so deep
I tap my toes to Beats.
The meter is mostly 4--3
That makes for the two lines.

I like Quatrains, a group—four lines
That makes a Stanza true.
We use a space to separate
One stanza from the next.

By now the meters very set
The words they come 4--3.
Don't have to think, that's how they come
I only write them down.

I must remember Syllables
To end the line correctly.
The beats must come 4--3, 4--3
Can't have a hanger-on.

Don't try for Metaphors and such
Similes I use bit more.
Rhyme just happens when they do
Don't really try to do.

I usually dwell in story-time
It's called a Narrative.
Some say I write in what's Blank Verse
But without all that rhyme.

When I begin to write a poem
I don't know where it's going.
Sometimes a thought will enter in
And change the compass point.

Most stanzas number six, eight or twelve
I really never know.
Some thoughts are long, some thoughts are short
But all must find an end.

The last stanza must wrap it up
Must bring it to an end.
It must conclude the thought in mind
And let the reader rest.

I let this poem go some more lines
To let you know how I
Don't have to struggle finding words.
This has been a half an hour.

When words come out they flow to me
My mind's a busy place.
I hardly ever edit poems
They are complete to me.

Glen Wasson
October 31, 2023

#831
Working With Words

A poets day is never dull
Because he's working with words.
The building blocks of all we say
And all of history.

Each word will have some meaning
To help explain the world.
To clarify, exemplify
To bring it into view.

To some the world is blurry
The focus is not clear.
But learning words can clear that up
And now it has some meaning.

Words are mighty, functional too
They make the world make sense.
To see as you have never seen,
To open up your eyes.

Words can fill a library
And spread on T.V. waves.
We all take part in using them
They are a part of us.

Each day with open mouths we speak
The words we need to share.
With one and all we freely say
The words that must be spoken.

A poet's never tongue-tied,
He always has a word.
To share with all both young and old
And bring their life some joy.

A happy smile, a word or two
Will often lift a day,
To lighten someones darkened soul
That life has trampled down.

Words are tools that poets use
To freely share their thoughts.
To lift a life or cause a thought
To enter in your mind.

Words, words, words, words
They're all we have to use.
What better thing to spread around
A useful medium.

Glen Wasson
November 2, 2023

#832
Spirits

Is there a spirit hanging round
No, not the Holy one.
Just one that sort of floats around
And gathers close to you.

Who doesn't come on strong at all
Seems he's a gentle type.
From time to time you know he's there
And all without a reason.

You can't see them, only sense
They're always in the background.
But sometimes they will gather in
And give your arms a tingle.

They really never touch you
You know when they are near.
Sometimes it's comforting to know
They keep an eye on you.

Mostly the feelings good to have
A bit of calm and peace.
Occasionally a chill will come
And cause you to reflect.

Perhaps it is the nudge you need
To straighten out your life.
A sort of wake-up-call you get
Of things that are not clear.

Are spirits real? I've not sensed one
I'm speaking from my mind.
But many people that I know
Believe that they exist.

The church may say I'm out of line
To write about a spirit.
But thoughts within my mind speak out
To write what I've been thinking.

While some may say "They're bad, they're good"
I feel they are benign.
Someone may feel a comfort from
These airy, unseen spirits.

Glen Wasson
November 2, 2023

#833
Fall

It's nine o-clock and the air is brisk
It's November 3rd and Fall.
The sky is blue in Yuma town
Almost like every day.

While snow is falling in places north
A jacket or sweater is fine.
Shorts and tee shirts rule the day
No need to change too soon.

Summers are hot—monsoon brings rain
We wait for the month of October.
Snowbirds return, the heat has backed off
Waiting for Yumas winter.

November through March, the graceful time
Warmer than those up north.
No snow or ice to hinder your way
Just gentle sun every day.

The R.V. Parks are filling now
They don't want to be stopped by snow.
Yuma's thought of as hot and dry
And that is mostly true.

Two—three inches of rain each year
The river flows nearby.
But water wets the nearby fields
And grows the bountiful crops.

Known history goes to 1540
But natives many more.
Not just a wide spot in the road
We are a destination.

Enjoy your days in Yuma town
Mi casa, su casa, your town
Enjoy our little town.

Glen Wasson
November 3, 2023

#834
Food and Drink

Food and drink are needed more
But not as much as air and water.
Clothing's nice if it gets too cold
But in the end we all exist.

We don't all life on a tropic ile
Some have even some ice and snow.
Our needs may change as we move around
The earth is huge but we are spaced out.

The poles are covered with ice so thick
Yet at the equator the sun is hot.
And people live from pole to pole
Causing need for modes of dress.

Someone must hunt the meat to eat
And others must gather the fruits and nuts.
And others must do all the rest to be done
Together it needs a village and more.

Glen Wasson
November 3, 2023

#835
Reading a Book

Just spent some time reading a book
About the art of poetry.
Not by a poet like you and me
But one who teaches the art.

Who teaches college students fare
And also children small.
A published poet, several books
And known the world wide.

While using words to me quite strange
She seemed so far away.
New York and other lofty sites
I could not understand.

She spoke of poems as something high
Complex beyond my mind.
My simple poems are clear to me
I feared to take hers in.

She spoke of poetry circles
I am a lone poet.
No-one wants to gather in
And analyze a poem.

My many friends want one or two
Perhaps to be polite.
But strokes the ego in my soul
I'll write another day.

Glen Wasson
November 5, 2023

#836
Flowing Words

It's fur A.M. And words are flowing
Can't sleep so I am up.
Reading a bit bout poetry
Now writing the words that come.

I love the flow of words that come
Whenever that may be.
Don't make them up, they come to me
So easy to write down.

My thoughts of life and all
Suggest an active mind.
Have no control how will work out
I merely float along.

But words contained in lines like these
Are all I care about.
My heart and mind and soul alive
I trust the words that come.

Don't need to force them out right now
The come with effort nil.
Enjoy it when the time is right,
That's poetry to me.

Glen Wasson
November 5, 2023
4 A.M.

#837
Saturday Night at the Coffee Bean

Saturday night at the Coffee Bean
It happens first and third.
We gather round, bout ten or twelve
To play and sing and read.

There's guitars, flutes and fiddles too
Harmonicas, even ukes.
To play and sing and bring some joy
I read a poem or two.

Some are just old rockers
They're heydays were back then
Now it's mostly fun and games
But some find a gig or two.

Saturday night is just for fun
To keep the fingers loose.
To be a memory next week
And recollect the fun.

We get to play, two—three, and one
Depending on the time.
Sometimes we have a couple more
And have to keep it short.

A few of the younger folk show up
The newer generation.
Don't always know the older songs
The rockers like to play.

But all in all we're happy folk
Enjoying a fun night out.
Two weeks from now we'll meet again
And rock around the clock.

Glen Wasson
November 5, 2023

#838
What Kind of Poetry do I Write

I write poetry in a mostly traditional way. I use meter, feet and line breaks but very little rhyme. Unlike modern Free Verse I use modified Blank Verse in that it is rhythm based but without a rhyme scheme. Where Free Verse has no rules I have self imposed rules of how I write:

- I like my poems to flow and march the whole length.
- I like four line Stanzas.
- I like my poems to be Narratives that tell a story, beginning, middle, end.
- Most of my poems begin when I get a single thought or phrase.
- I write without profanity.
- I stare each line with a capital letter.
- My Stanzas consist of 4—3, 4—3 beats.
- I edit as I write in my journal and as I type into the computer.
- While I don't often deviate from my form, I will from time to time chose a different meter or interesting form as an experiment.

Glen Wasson
November 7, 2023

#839

Age

Is it a noun or a verb?
A name or an action?

As we live our lives we age a lot,
Until we reach "That age."

Throughout history there have been many ages:
- The Stone Age
- The Bronze Age
- The Iron Age

Mankind has lived through them all
And as they lived through them they aged.

Ever been told to "Act your age!"
Age is just a number.

At what age are we an adult?
Is "Aged man." an adjective?

When do we reach "Old age."
Do we fight aging?
Is age the same as old?

Be careful how you reach it,
This subject we call age.
It may be just a number,
But people still are counting.

Glen Wasson
November 7, 2023

#840
A Yawn

Have you ever had to yawn
Like your lower jaw would break?
Where your mouth is wide and your throat is too
Did you cover your mouth as shy?

Did you ever have to yawn
When someone yawned before you?
Why does that happen?
Why are they contagious?

Did you ever yawn before someone
Just to make them yawn?
Did you tell them you were sorry
Or just an evil grin?

Do all animals yawn?
I know dogs and cats do.
Did you ever see a cow yawn
Or weren't you even looking?

Why do we say we're sorry
Did you give someone offense?
Are we sorry or just embarrassed?
Why do we even care?

Yawning is just so natural
We do it every day.
A natural function of our lives
Offensive as a fart?

Glen Wasson
November 7, 2023

#840
The Sun

The sun shines hot on my face
My arms and legs are not.
The breeze sucks all the warmth from them
Why don't they feel the heat?

I sit in my chair relaxing
Enjoying the morning sun.
Retirement means relaxing
No work that must be done.

At eighty-four I feel I've earned
This time I now enjoy.
I sleep and eat, relax and write
These are the Golden Years.

I could live up north in cold
But my abode is Yuma.
Blue sky, green trees and winters warm
No snow or ice to bear.

While I live here the whole year round
Many come for now.
Take in our hospitality
And stay for several months.

For me I'll stay for summer
Partake the heat that's day.
And age another year in life
This place that I call home.

Glen Wasson
November 9, 2023

#842
My Hood

Blue sky, green trees, concrete walls
Adorn my neighborhood.
Parking lots with asphalt paved
And striped for parking stalls.

With nearby trees the pigeons come
Quite often two by two.
Is food, or what, they're looking for
Why not then seek the grass?

Today is windy, quite a bit
The sun though feels so good.
Find a spot without the wind
Enjoy November day.

Within the courtyard two trees were
Removed with saws so sharp.
The others doing not so well
Looks like they need more water.

People roam around this place
Where senior people live.
We're past our prime, now live sublime
Enjoying what is left.

While others get up, go to work
We all prepare for coffee.
Some orange juice, French toast, sausage too
Our way to start the day.

Old age is different than back then
When worked until you died.
We feel we've put in all our time
Now other things to do.

We have three hots, a cot and bath
Two rooms in which to live.
A courtyard to enjoy in time
With other things to do.

With staff to care for most our needs
We gently live our lives.
We hope it is a gentle slope
Not looking for the end.

With everyone as old as us
From time to time they leave.
Reminded that life can be that short
Give thanks for what we have.

Give thanks for what we have in life
We live a blessed life.
Enjoy each others company
May be all we have.

Glen Wasson
November 9, 2023

#843
Fall and the
Snowbirds

This morning's just like all the rest
Blue sky, no clouds, cool breeze.
It's fall in our own Yuma town
It's just like all the rest.

We're spoilt round here as winter comes
That special time in Yuma.
When everyone from way up north
Comes down to spend the winter.

Is there ice up where you live
There is none in my Yuma.
Do you ever shovel snow
You wouldn't here in Yuma.

You'll need tee shirts and shorts to wear
And have a like for sunshine.
Both are common for my town
It's really pretty nice.

I'm sitting with both shoes removed
While sitting at my desk.
Don't spend a lot of time outside
But many others do.

There's things to do in Yuma town
And many R.V. Parks.
There's swimming, sunning—golf to play
And other things to do.

While snow drifts deep back home up north
You'll visit our Old Town.
That's down where Yuma started from
With little shops to visit.

Now prison hill is quite a site
Jail cells when things got bad.
You'll visit now when things get cool
And think when things were hot.

From there you'll see the river flow
And watch canoes and tubes.
And swimmers going in and out
Not something done back home.

Come be a Snowbird here in town
And all surrounding too.
You'll have a respite from the snow
And work upon your tan.

Glen Wasson
November 11, 2023

#844

Prose – How I Write Poetry

- How To Write Better Poetry in 10 Easy Steps
- 3 Ways To Get Started Writing Poetry
- Solving Writers Block in 10 Minutes
- Using Brain Maps

We've all seen the YouTube ads like above, you have a problem, here is the answer. Or Google "poetry help" and the screen erupts with ideas. While I have clicked on my fair amount, few have addressed my problems, or what I thought were my problems. We are all wanting to improve our work but I seem to be unique in that I don't experience those problems.

From an early age I experienced music and the rhythmic beats it lives by. As I aged I was in marching band, Air National Guard and Basic Training, all drilling into my mind counting beats, left – right, left – right, 1 – 2, 1 – 2,   1 – 2 – 3 – 4,   1 – 2 – 3 – 4. A lot of people can't count beats but I can.

I found poetry at 82 and never struggled with how mine developed, it just came to me, I never had to hunt for it. I never have writers block as I just wait for the words to come and write. I have no writing ritual or set time.

I am comfortable writing about life, the weather or my surroundings. For me the first thing I need is a line or phrase, dwell upon it for a while or get out of bed and write. If the time is right the words just come in four line stanzas called Quatrains. They often come in 4 – 3, 4 – 3 beats per Quatrain. I have set this as a standard for me as I am comfortable with it. I don't look for rhymes, just meter.

I print it out by hand in my Journal #4, editing words as I go. This will take me about half an hour for a normal twelve stanza poem. It ends when it ends. After this I type it into the computer and use spellcheck and revise a bit more. That is the end of my editing. It is now ready for publication online and to my living community.

I write from my life experiences which are unique. I was born in 1939 in a small Nebraska town. Growing up we moved many times, attending six schools before graduating high school. As an adult I continued moving, now having over 55 addresses and 35 jobs. After graduating I began my 40 year engineering career as a Drafting Trainee and progressing to Mechanical Engineer, all without a degree. My last job at Boeing encouraged me to complete my degree where I obtained my BS Degree in Total Quality Management in 1999 when I retired.

As you can see I was a "Thing" person, having no use for the Liberal Arts. This changed in 2019, at the age of 80 when I began taking online classes in Literature and Philosophy, completing over 60 classes. In February 2021 I took my first class in Poetry and never looked back. I am now a "People" person anxious to meet and greet people and make friends. I now reside in a Senior Living community with my new wife, Michelle.

I published my first book, *New Poetry by an Old Man,* in July 2021 and am preparing a second one in the near future.

#188 - A New Beginning

Leaves softly blowing in the breeze
Blown by a gentle, gentle breeze.
Moving light and shadow all in time
A random always going on.

The sun is setting behind me
The light before is quickly leaving.
Thoughts are thinking of the coming eve
Day is almost over, almost over.

The sunspots are almost gone
The leaves become more quiet.
Sunset is a quiet time of day
As darkness envelops the scene.

In twelve hours the scene will be reversed
The sun coming in the windows east.
The light will overcome the dark
A new beginning of a brand new day.

Glen Wasson
May 18, 2021

#848
Yuma Sky

The Yuma sky is blue today
So like the other days.
No clouds are seen in all the sky
Would bore if not so nice.

It's late in the year as winter comes
The Snowbirds flock to town.
They flee the cold they leave up north
Relish in what they find.

We are unique in what we have
Invites so many in.
We who live here all year round
Enjoy the winter too.

What goes on in the fields out there
Feeds many through the winter.
Two hundred thousand acres worth
Is worked throughout the year.

Though summer temps are very hot
We still enjoy it here.
It's not so crowded when they're gone
The pace slows down a bit.

Blue sky's ours the whole year round
We're blessed to have it so.
Enjoy our town in every way
Enjoy our Yuma town.

Glen Wasson
November 19, 2023

#849
The Weather

It must have rained last night
There's puddles on the sidewalk.
I didn't hear it rain last night
While I was lightly sleeping.

They say a storm is brewing
Somewhere out south and west,
Above the Sea Pacific
Beyond the shore we see.

But day brings blue filled sky
No clouds to break the view.
You'd think that it was summer
But eleventh month it is.

I live where snow is absent
And ice does not appear.
Where sun shines almost every day
And storms are far between.

No chill will pass your shoulder
And comfort is the norm.
Look to the sky, it is so blue
Relax, enjoy the day.

If rain will stay in nighttime
While I remain in bed,
I will reply with poem in hand
Salute it in its stead.

Glen Wasson
November 19, 2023

#850
I Learned

Last Saturday night I learned

I speak before I think

And that other people

Don't like to be called old

Glen Wasson
November 19, 2023

#851
Friends

Friends—those you hold close to you
They're more like they are blood.
Closer than some who are really blood
They mean so much to you.

They come into your life at times
Unlike those who come by birth,
But like your own relation ones
Can wait for years to meet.

At eighty-four I have few friends,
The ones that you hold close.
Have many I say "Hi" to
But few that I hold close.

But that's O.K., I've lived a lot
And moved around the world.
Few I've known are still around
Next year be fewer still.

Glen Wasson
November 20, 2023

#852
Senses

SIGHT

Oh, to see what I can't see
To find out I'm not blind.
To open my eyes to what's out front
To open them up to light.

To see what I can't see
May seem a bit obscure
But all are blind in little things
Don't look for things to change.

SOUND

Sometimes we're deaf to things we hear
We cover our ears with hands
Or say "La, la, la, la, la, la"
To drown out all we fear.

TASTE/SPEECH

But yet our tongues are not restrained
They never cease to wag.
Why don't we bite our tongues to stop
The Babble they put forth.

SMELL   When faced with smells that we dislike
         Our wrinkled nose says "Phew."
         What we don't like some others may
         It is a personal thing.

TOUCH   You ever pull your hand right back
         From one you see as "Dirty?"
         Or draw away from a hot stove
         For fear of being burned?

         Our senses say so much bout us
         For all the world to see.
         They are how we perceive the world
         And what it means to us.

         They praise us and they curse us
         It's always up to us.
         To keep a bridle on all five
         And put a face on it.

         To hear no evil, say none too
         To see all that is good.
         A good way to begin the day
         To start out with good thoughts.

         Hold out your hand to help them up
         The ones we see in need.
         To say we're not in need of help
         Is lying to ourselves.

         If not for God that could be us
         We have no room to brag.
         With grace and luck we are ourselves
         Was not all from our effort.

Glen Wasson
November 21, 2023

#853
The Pain of Writing

Oh, what does it mean to write
Put words upon a page.
To open your mind and let words flow
And share your pain with others.

By pain I mean with effort
It could be bad or good.
To search for love and find it
May be a tiring trip.

But was it worth the effort
Expended to achieve?
The far elusive destiny
That love will give to you.

To write a poem may make you work
Your heart, your mind, your soul.
But when they work together they
Produce the poetry.

Glen Wasson
November 22, 2023

#854
Use The Day

What use is a day if it's not put to use
If it's not pursued with vigor.
If it's left to float by like a passing cloud
Not noticed for what it could be.

Be it good, be it bad, it is not left to us
But it is up to us what we make it to be.
We are not in this life to be making a mess
But to generate good and give forth all we have.

All our culture comprises what we all have done
A collective of everyone's input and work.
All our lives put together makes culture appear.
It's certainly not left to you or to me.

Today I'll contribute whatever I can
And give forth from my heart, my mind and my soul.
It may be the last time I'm given to give
Must leave on a positive note when I go.

Glen Wasson
November 25, 2023